The World of Shakespeare and his Contemporaries

The World of Shakespeare and his Contemporaries

A Visual Approach

by

Maurice Hussey

EMBLEM deduceth conceptions intellectual
to images sensible, and that which is
sensible more easily imprinted than that
which is intellectual.
FRANCIS BACON

HEINEMANN
LONDON

Heinemann Educational Books Ltd
LONDON EDINBURGH MELBOURNE AUCKLAND TORONTO
HONG KONG SINGAPORE KUALA LUMPUR NEW DELHI
NAIROBI JOHANNESBURG LUSAKA IBADAN
KINGSTON

ISBN 0 435 18463 6 (paperback)

For John Tyler

Set in Lumitype Janson 11 pt, 1 pt leaded and
printed on Mellotex Smooth Super White

Published by
Heinemann Educational Books Ltd
48 Charles Street, London W1X 8AH

Printed in Great Britain by
Butler & Tanner Ltd, Frome and London

Contents

Acknowledgements

I am principally indebted to those who have helped in a variety of ways with the locating, taking or processing of the illustrations. The Photographer of the Cambridge University Library (Mr G. Rawlings) and the Visual Aids Officer of the College of Arts and Technology, Cambridge (Mr B. S. Clarke) have each been most kind. The staff of Heinemann Educational Books have assisted in a hundred ways and deserve recognition. My friend, Surendra Agarwala, has driven me many miles in search of likely material for this book from Fountains Abbey in the north to the coast of Amalfi in the south where, in spite of Webster's dramatic declaration, we found no sign of a Duchess.

For the right to reproduce copyright material we are indebted to the following: Radio Times Hulton Picture Library (Fig. Nos. 1, 53); Royal Commission on Historical Monuments (4, 5, 6a, 6c, 8, 36, 128, 136); Royal Commission on Historical Monuments and Hon. Society of the Middle Temple (43); Surendra Agarwala (6b, 7, 22, 136); Walter Scott, Bradford (9); Reece Winstone (10); Lord Salisbury of Hatfield House (11); Ian Barker (13, 112); British Museum (15, 35, 40, 42, 69, 95, 116, 118, 132); The Courtauld Institute (16, 55a, 55b, 55c, 55d, 63, 78); The Courtauld Institute and the Provost and Fellows of Worcester College, Oxford (51); The Courtauld Institute and Losely Estate for the More-Molyneux Collection (85, 109); The Courtauld Institute and the Trustees of the Chatsworth Settlement—Devonshire Collection (130, 133, 135); Fitzwilliam Museum, Cambridge (32, 49); National Gallery (41, 48, 70); Bibliothèque Royale, Brussels (44, 106, 120); Utrecht University Library (46); Commune di Vicenza (50); Philadelphia Museum of Art: W. P. Wilstach Collection (57); Edward Leigh (61, 67, 131); Victoria and Albert Museum (64); Cambridge University Press (68); Musée des Beaux Arts, Brussels (74, 91, 126); Alte Pinakothek, Munich (76): National Portrait Gallery (82, 83, 100, 114, 140); Danish Tourist Board (93); Dulwich College Picture Library (94); Director of Venice Art Gallery (97); Bodleian Library, Oxford (123a, 127); Ashmolean Museum, Oxford (123b, 141); National Museum of Art, Copenhagen (137); Country Life (139); Professor Glynne Wickham for his map of 'The City of London' c. 1600 (page 42). All other illustrations in the text are reproduced by permission of the Cambridge University Library.

THE UNTON PANORAMA
(*unknown*, 1557–96)
Front and back endpapers

The personal and diplomatic activities of SIR HENRY UNTON of Wadley, Berkshire, and Oriel College, Oxford, provide, thanks to an anonymous and presumably Flemish artist, the best surviving Elizabethan panorama. His birth in 1557, his education and travels in Italy, the Low Countries and France, the scene of his death in 1596 form several parts of this panorama. The right-hand section is dominated by the ceremonies attendant upon his wedding with its masque of Diana and Mercury, its string consort upstairs and its mixed or 'broken' one downstairs consisting of flute, cittern, treble and bass viols, pandora lute sustained by a drummer on the platform who may also have been a singer. The funeral procession dominates its own part of the whole.

The trumpeting angel, the call of death and even the ornate chimneys are all calculated to encircle the personal world in that of emblem and to sustain it with the quality of national and supernatural life as the artist imagined it.

The panorama is reproduced by permission of the National Portrait Gallery.

Preface

This volume is intended as an unusual and attractive step towards the understanding of some of the best-known plays of Shakespeare, Marlowe and Jonson as well as countless other works of their period. The illustrations assembled from many sources in several countries show us some of the common assumptions of educated people in Tudor and Stuart England and attempt to focus them in works of literature as well as providing visual delight.

All readers of Shakespeare are aware that he employs the technique of metaphor and symbol in his plays, drawing upon such fields as the planetary system, the human body in health and disease, the animal world, and the sophisticated backgrounds of court and theatre, among others, for his purpose. His method was also instinctively followed by Marlowe and Jonson though their imaginative worlds were often more bookish. To understand a great deal of this language, however, no formal education was needed since it came from the environment. To provide some notes on some major Renaissance symbols is the purpose of these packed pages.

In her own way Queen Elizabeth drew upon various sources of symbolism for the projection of her own ego. As was made clear from the Elizabethan exhibition at the Tate Gallery, London, in early 1970, her range of images was precise and stylized. Uppermost in her mind were symbols of virginity and chastity: the eglantine or wild white rose; the ermine; the sieve, associated with the Roman Vestal Virgins. She imagined herself an incarnation of Diana, the goddess of the crescent moon, hunting and chastity; or Astraea, the deity of justice, together with her symbol of the sword. On other occasions she invited her people to see her as the phoenix, unique and chaste, or the pelican, mother of her English children, loving and self-sacrificing. Portraits of her show the rainbow or olive branch of peace, the crowned pillar of constancy, and globes terrestrial or celestial to depict majesty in microcosm and macrocosm, while spring flowers had the meaning of the eternal spring that accompanied the return of the legendary Golden Age under her aegis.

Some of these images appear later in the book as part of the visual store of our ancestors in their compact and largely triumphant island. As we study them in their dramatic contexts we shall come to appreciate that a picture can be quite as convincing a way of realizing an abstract concept as a word; both of them can change in nuance over a long period. For many of us the symbolic meaning of these pictures may be quite obscure but once the idiom has been grasped the whole language comes alive. To help the modern reader towards an interpretation of both image and idea extending far beyond my own pages is my intention in this book.

M. P. H.
April 1971

1 *Unknown Artist*, Elizabeth I *(c. 1600). Eye-ear motif
symbolizes Fame; the rainbow, Peace; the Serpent,
Wisdom.*

1. The Country Displayed

Most people today are familiar with the *icon* as a holy picture with a golden background standing behind an altar. It is not in this sense of the word that it is used hereafter but as an over-riding image, secular or sacred, implying and demanding the spectator's acceptance, endorsement and, where necessary, veneration. It may be of a person or an institution, a monarch, a deity, or a corporate idea like a city. The portraits of Queen Elizabeth (1) were always of this type, emblems of her autocratic rule, propaganda pictures rather than realistic portrayals. Indeed, as she approached and passed the climacteric age of nine times seven years she saw to it that a portrait was imperious and theatrical with little of the truth about it. 'At 50', wrote George Orwell, 'every one has the face he deserves.' It was as if Elizabeth accepted this epigram in advance. Thus she would be Astraea, goddess of justice; or Dian(a), goddess of hunting and chastity; Head of the Church; or Head of State. From the assiduity with which she culti-

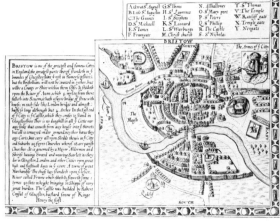

2 (below left) *Michael Drayton*, Polyolbion *(1612). Gloucestershire, an imaginative survey.*

3a (above) *John Speed*, Theatre of Empire *(1611), Bristol*

vated herself as the Virgin Queen, especially in her later non-nubile days, one feels sure that, Protestant or no, she would have had no qualms at being mistaken pictorially for the Virgin Mary.

There was no specifically Elizabethan countryside; it was merely open space more copiously wooded than our own. Therefore, with its comic apparatus of river-nymphs, sheep-grazing and crop-husbandry, consider the slightly post-Elizabethan map (2). The feasting and revelry of the Cotswold Games were forcefully revived by James but fit a medieval pattern, as do the maps (3a, 3b) of the main ports and cities of Bristol and Norwich which handled the export trade in English wool and cloth, our major source of stability at a time when more speculative voyages pursuing the "naughtiness of the silver" occasioned economic miseries at home.

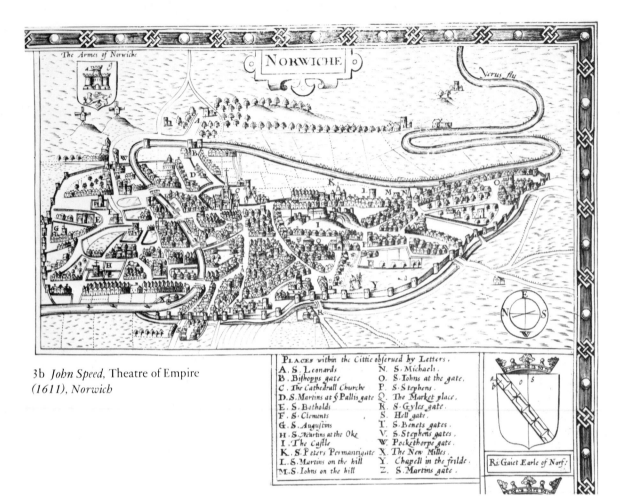

3b *John Speed,* Theatre of Empire
(1611), Norwich

PLACES within the Cittie obferued by Letters.
A . S . Leonards
B . Bifhopps gate
C . The Cathedrall Churche
D.S.Martins at ý Pallis gate
E . S . Botholds
F . S . Clements
G. S . Augufins
H . S . Martins at the Oke
I . The Caftle
K . S . Peters Permanrigate
L . S . Martins on the hill
M . S . Iohns on the hill

N . S . Michaels .
O . S . Iohns at the gate.
P . S . Stephens .
Q . The Market place .
R . S . Gyles gate .
S . Hell gate .
T . S . Benets gates .
V . S . Stephens gates .
W . Pockethorpe gate .
X . The New Milles .
Y . Chapell in the frilde .
Z . S . Martins gate .

R: Gaiet Earle of Norf:

4 (below) *Aldeburgh, Suffolk: Moot Hall (c. 1530). Note
blend of brick and timber and the chimneys.*

Social historians have singled out the great re-
building projects of later Elizabethan days. They
affected both town and village with results, largely
lost, but much sought by the modern visitor. In
York or in Canterbury, for instance, such remnants
are numerous, and in the counties on the border
of Wales one has only to search for an hour to discover the black-and-white 'Magpie houses'. These
are remarkable for their aesthetic qualities with
naked black timbers which are both the soul and
skeleton of the building and totally indispensable.
Old carpentry and craftsmanship can be instantly
contrasted with modern pseudo-Tudor imitations
in which the beams are hauled into place after the
operations, only wafer-thin and merely for show.

One of the gems among English public buildings is the small Moot Hall at Aldeburgh, erected
in the reign of Henry VIII (4), while another

which is especially attractive is the Feathers Inn in Ludlow (5). The first of these was built to house the administration of a small coastal town and the other to serve inland traffic which increased sharply towards 1600 when, for the first time, everything seemed to run on wheels. So fine an inn as this would have been bank, court and post office as well as hotel, warehouse and coach park.

English people, for whatever reasons, have long been obsessed with buildings such as those above and unusually nostalgic in all their art about country life. The ideal pattern seems to have been the one that Shakespeare himself took: work in the town after a childhood in the country and make enough money to return in superior circumstances to the grass roots. Those who had large manors were not content till they were extended. Where once a central hall was all that was required, then, to the irritation of moralists, there spread a pursuit of privacy out of which came small rooms called parlours (to talk in) and further bedrooms above the hall. No longer did the gentry want to conduct so much of their life in public if they could

5 (left) Ludlow, Shropshire: Feathers Inn (1603). Asymmetry intensified by the lozenge-patterns and the balcony.

6a Longleat, Wiltshire (1586 onwards), 'the most regular building in the kingdom', designed by Robert Smythson.

6b (above) *Castle Ashby, Northamptonshire (rebuilt 1574 onwards). Façade by Inigo Jones. This county was noteworthy for newly settled rich landowners.*

6c *Fountains Hall, Yorkshire (1601 onwards). Height accentuated by hillside site, it looks down on Fountains Abbey, immense ruins.*

afford to build upwards and sideways. In the end the first floor became the 'noble floor', as it was in Italy, and the downstairs hall was demoted to the status of an entrance pleased to be the location of a great stairway out of it.

In studying any of the architectural pictures it is always wise to consider the skyline to see what miscellaneous gables and turrets were assembled there. Ben Jonson, the dramatist whose evidence we often hereafter quote, had been a bricklayer in his youth and later a connoisseur of the Golden Age of the Feudal Hall. He was a visitor at Pens-

hurst Place in Kent, birthplace of Sir Philip Sidney:

> Thou art not, Penshurst, built to envious show.
> Of touch or marble, nor canst thou boast a row
> Of polished pillars or a roof of gold:
> Thou hast no lantern whereof tales are told;
> Or stair, or courts, but stand'st an ancient pile.
> (Jonson, 'To Penshurst')

7 *Rushton,*
Northamptonshire,
Triangular Lodge (1579).
Architectural conceit
devised by Sir Thomas
Tresham. Each face is 33 ft.
4 ins. wide.

8 *Stokesay Castle, Shropshire. Gatehouse (c. 1610). Example of Border building style in oak and yellowish plaster.*

9 (below) *Wilmcote, Warwickshire. Mary Arden's House. Outstanding example of early sixteenth-century farmhouse, fortunately open to the public.*

A modern visitor encounters a hall that Chaucer may have known, with banners and a hall-screen, but sees further courts from the intervening centuries.* For Jonson Penshurst symbolized the Good Life while more modern mansions were to their owners Commodity, Firmness and Delight but status-symbols as well. Feasting or 'housekeeping' of the old pattern gave Jonson the utmost pleasure and the reactionary in him feared lest the culture of the country-house hospitality might fade away and civilized intercourse go with it.

Longleat (6a) is the earliest of these three houses and Fountains (6c) the latest, but all large buildings were in continuous evolution inside and out. Castle Ashby (6b) has a series of Latin inscriptions all round invoking divine protection, and one is pursued into the grounds with an unsuitable text (added later) on the modesty of the 'lilies of the fields'. All such renaissance buildings demand to be *read* in one way or another, but Fountains has to be understood intuitively. Beside it lies the despoiled ruin of Fountains Abbey, the largest monastic relic in Europe, from which the stones were carried away to put up the undeniably beautiful Hall, the home of Sir Stephen Proctor, about whose greed nobody has had a good word to say.

*For a picture of Penshurst see *The Age of Chaucer* (Pelican).

10 *Stanton, Gloucestershire. Limestone cottages preserved (early twentieth century) to retain Elizabethan character and dignity of village.*

But, hardly a Renaissance poem ventures to comment on the disappearence of all our monasteries, an absence difficult to justify.

No doubt there are continental ideas embodied in these buildings, but in the sphere of the country house English masonry, carpentry and other crafts reached unexpected heights. One of the oddest of all is the totally triplicate Triangular Lodge built by Sir Thomas *Tres*ham in honour of the Trinity at his home in Northamptonshire (7), a county in which three-quarters of the landowners were of recent origin and all energetic builders. This is a literary-architectural conceit to be read, without precedent overseas. Another contemporary highlight is the free-standing gatehouse at Stokesay Castle, not far from Ludlow (8). Originally a fortified castle needed a defended gatehouse, but this was not one of them. It is the ideal spot for a Porter, as in *Macbeth*, to keep a bleary eye on people passing in and out. On a much humbler level but equally distinguished are Mary Arden's House at Wilmcote, the home of Shakespeare's mother (9), and the dignified, calm and square-mullioned Cotswold cottages (10). Beauty and craftsmanship have in them created a good place to live in without the advantages of great wealth.

William Harrison, collaborator of the noted chronicler Holinshed, wrote what is the completest account of the state of England in mid-Elizabethan times. One of his observations was of the crop of elaborate chimneys, called by the satirist, John Hall, 'the wind-pipes of good fellowship'. It was the phenomenon Shakespeare worked into *Henry IV*, Part I ('Charles's wain is over the new chimney') and also into *Henry VI*. The bizarre style, already noticeable over the Aldeburgh Moot Hall, is there principally for self-advertisement and was affected by householders of all ranks as a new craze when earlier the same people had made do with much less prominent air-vents. Harrison also testified to the interior decorations which were likewise growing more elaborate. Tapestries with all manner of foliage, blossom and animal life worked into them, originating either in Flanders or in English workshops, were highly prized. Shakespeare offers just such another anachronistic image in *Cymbeline* with its masquerade of his favourite icons and a piece of self-quotation:

> tapestry of silk and silver: the story,
> Proud Cleopatra when she met her Roman.
> . . . and the chimneypiece
> Chaste Dian bathing.

We meet here the delight in the risqué and the mythological which recurs throughout Renaissance literature. In the prologue to *The Taming of the Shrew* the anonymous Lord has a collection of 'wanton pictures' such as stand out in the canvases, panel-paintings and tapestries of the day. Our example (11) is crowded with natural life and fertility but quite innocuous.

Though Castle Ashby, for instance, now has a formal Augustan garden layout by Capability Brown, it originally possessed a small Dutch herb and flower garden with numerous plants. A typical gardening-book of the day advised owners on the layout of mazes (12), an art developed at Hatfield House and Hampton Court. Mazes were from the earliest times capable of being interpreted as symbols of human difficulties, adding visual charms at the same time.

In general, Harrison was perfectly justified to praise 'in these our years wherein our woodmen excel and are in manner comparable in skill with old Vitruvius, Leo Baptista [Alberti] and Serlo.' The influential architect he had apparently not heard of was Andrea Palladio, whose Villa Rotonda at Vicenza (13) with its four identical faces, pilasters and stucco-work is unthinkable in Elizabethan England. However, that villa is a portent of the eighteenth century when, against great opposition, the classically proportioned country house was suddenly planted here by a group of distinguished architects who belatedly discovered the Palladian ideal, and worked at Chiswick, Holkham Hall and elsewhere.

It would be a mistake to concentrate entirely upon the physical concomitants of Elizabethan civilization. Samuel Daniel, the poet, seems to have foreseen the triumph of the literature which grew out of his world:

> who, in time, knows, whither we may vent
> The treasure of our tongue, to what strange
>   shores
> This gain of our best glory shall be sent?
> (Daniel, 'Musophilus')

11 *Hatfield House, Hertfordshire*: Autumn *(c. 1611)*
one of set of seasonal tapestries crowded with fertility,
dominated by god and zodiac.

13 (above) *Vicenza, Villa Rotonda (1550) by Andrea Palladio. His perfect rhythm and symmetry in country-house building waited till the eighteenth century to be adopted as Palladianism in England.*

12 (right) *T. Hill, First Garden Book (1563). A maze, 'proper adornment upon pleasure to a garden', with smug owner.*

One of the most immediate semi-dramatic literary adjuncts of that country-house culture was the summer entertainment devised for the visit of the Queen. In towns she might expect a pageant of industry, in universities a learned dispute and a Latin play; in the country mansion what a wealth of amateur dramatics she witnessed. E. K. Chambers noted that there might be 'a sibyl lurking in every courtyard and gateway, a satyr in the boscage in every park' when she arrived. If she sat to eat, music would strike up, the very cake might be fashioned in the guise of Troy. She is thought to have been fond of water-shows and not to have minded those embarrassing water-gardens where the guests are suddenly drenched. Even so, the imagination boggles before a Hercules statue whose sole 'thing' was to urinate a spray of water over those present! When there were speeches somebody had to write them, with any amount of planning, preparation and exhaustion. In 1591 the Queen witnessed the outstanding water-pageant at Elvetham (14) in Hampshire. She was pursued to the pond with gifts and watched the water-nymphs in their revels from a waterside throne.

A CEREMONIAL SPATIAL POEM IN HONOUR OF THE QUEEN DISPLAYED DURING ONE OF HER PROGRESSES

Her Majestie, for Many Parts in her most Noble and Vertuous Nature to be found, resembleth to the Spire.

(Ye must begin beneath, according to the nature of the Device)

```
                    S k i e

                   Azured
                   In the
                   Assur'de

                 And better
                 And richer
                 Much greater

              Crownandempir
              After an hier
              For  to  aspire
              Like flame of fire
              In  form  of  Spire

           To   mount  on  hie
           Con - ti - nu - al - ly
           With  travel  and  teen,
           Most  gracious  Queen
           Ye  have  made  a  vow
           Shews  plainly  how
           Not  fained  but  true
           To   everyman's   vew
           Shining  cleere  in  you
           Of  so  bright  an  hewe
           Even    thus    vertewe

        Vanish   out   of   sight
        Till  his  fine  top  be  quite
        To   taper   in   the   ayre
        Endevours  soft  and  faire,
        By   his   kindly   nature,
        Of  tall  comely  stature
        Like  as  this  faire  figure
```

Entertainments continued thus throughout her visit until at her departure the nymphs reappeared weeping in black. As the carriages swept down the drive her hosts, who could in theory claim for expenses, no doubt collapsed with fatigue and relief.

It was an imposition arising from Elizabeth's need to show herself for veneration and from curious parsimony in her domestic arrangements. Wherever she went the pageantry was repeated and a riot of visual imagery and poetry was prepared. In *A Midsummer Night's Dream* the inspiration for the following speech of Oberon's may well have been a water-pageant and nothing else:

14 (above) *Elvetham, Hampshire. Water Pageant for Queen Elizabeth (1591) with Ship Isle, Snail Mount and Fortress constructed in crescent moon-shaped pond in Queen's honour.*

15 *J. Visscher,* Long View of London *(1616). Two-dimensional plan over-burdened with churches on North Bank and showing Globe Theatre and Bear Baiting (Hope Theatre) on South Bank or Bankside.*

once I sat upon a promontory
And heard a mermaid, on a dolphin's back,
Uttering such dulcet and harmonious breath
That the rude sea grew civil at her song.

(Act II. ii)

In just this manner did the countryside collect all its financial and imaginative resources for a royal progress. The simpler people were not excluded and rustic pageants and speeches, about which we know, alas, virtually nothing, were also accepted by the Queen. Figuratively, all these playlets and dances were stops on the way to the Globe Theatre, the home of the most accomplished dramatic art ever furnished for an English audience.

London, a metropolis of nearly a quarter of a million souls, was extremely pressed for space, though this is not apparent in the Visscher view (15). The river dominates from this perspective and so do the church spires, giving an unusually ecclesiastical character to a city which was probably no more given to piety than any other. For the texture of the small houses, quite missing in Visscher, turn to the background of Hoefnagel's scene of South London (16). He may make it resemble a Flemish village but his countrymen were extremely familiar in England and provided most of our best paintings of the day. From his labelling (*The Fell Schipes* and *The Galley Füste*) Visscher seems a little out of touch with the language, but we are endlessly grateful for the realistic touch of any Flemish or Dutch artist on an English scene. We could only wish there had been still more to catch that moment when the outdoor improvised drama or the formal set speech moved nearer and nearer to the sphere of the drama proper. Then we might have had much more documentation of the pageantry of the streets with 'its participants riding ornately-caparisoned horses or marching before and behind the honoured personage . . . while wild men or whifflers capered about with torches and swords to clear a path.'* That path is one that we shall try to trace in the rest of the book. It will be devoted to a study of the work of three creative artists in the context of Elizabethan

society, and it will pass into the world of the Stuarts beyond the crucial date of 1603. It is no part of the present undertaking to review the political and social history of the country during those changing years, though a few comments will be thrown out. The world of the dramatists was not measured out by political events: it had its roots in the world of overarching external ideas and of

* Alice Venetsky. *Pageantry and the Elizabethan Stage.* p. 18.

morality, and in search of it the highly stylized and formalized education of the period will be investigated.

16 *J. Hoefnagel,* Marriage Feast at Bermondsey *(1569?). Artist is one of group by tree, extreme right, an early instance of the Flemish painter at work in this country.*

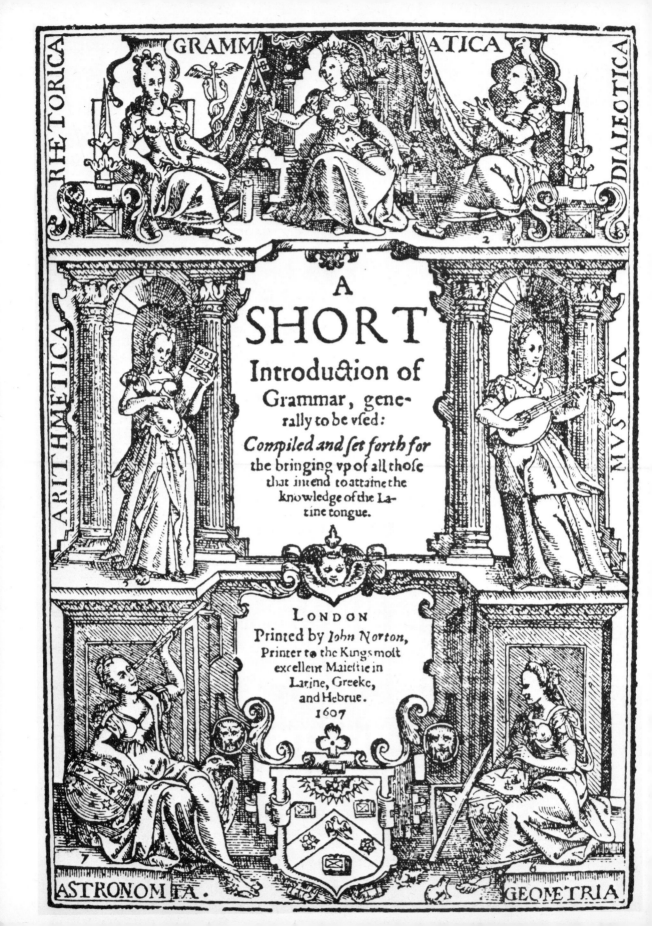

2. The Countries of the Mind

1 School: *Trivium*

There is no better image to head this section than the three sisters composing the medieval Trivium, explained by Thomas Wilson thus:

> GRAMMAR doth teach to utter words,
> To speak both apt and plain.
> LOGIC by art sets forth the truth
> And tells us what is vain.
> RHETORIC at large paints well the cause,
> And makes that seem right gay
> Which LOGIC spake but a word
> And taught as by the way.
>
> *(Rule of Reason)*

17 (left) *Anon*, Short Introduction to Grammar *(1607). Title-page with members of Trivium and Quadrivium symbolizing Arts courses.*

18 (above) *J. A. Comenius, Orbis Sensualium Pictus (1659). School picture showing the origin of 'forms' and two back-row boys who 'behave themselves wantonly' to invite ferula and rod on display.*

Schools founded by the medieval Church still provided the majority of young Elizabethans with their education but to them were added many founded by private individuals until over half the population was literate at the end of the reign. When, in later centuries, educational expansion was left to the reformed or state church one sees relative decline and a failure to keep pace with a growing population. Not until the 1902 Education Act was implemented, one imagines, was the cause as well served again.

Leaving aside the kindergarten or 'petty school', all education outside the family was concentrated upon Latin *Grammar* and literature. Thomas Nashe, on the whole a good advertisement for the system, remarked: 'Nouns and Pronouns, I pronounce you traitors to a boy's buttocks' and the grim seventeenth-century schoolroom (18) reinforces the lament. He and others between the ages of 7 and 15 or 16 in those free and fairly comprehensive boys' grammar schools learned to translate, analyse and compose Latin with a scattering of Greek in certain favoured towns.

Logic, or Dialectic, was patroness of academic disputations, oral and not written tests, which were the backbone of an education.

Rhetoric, daughter of Mercury, may be understood as the art of broadening and amplifying simple expression by the manipulation of tone and emotion in the words and giving outline and structure to an entire composition with judgement and verbal felicity. For a simple demonstration of the difference between the realms of these two sisters we may take the ancient emblem of the Open Palm of Rhetoric and the Clenched Fist of Logic.

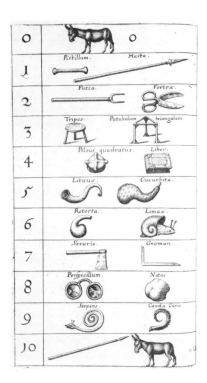

19 (left) *Robert Fludd*, Utriusque Cosmi . . . Historia *(1619). Table of numbers.*

20 (below) *W. Cunningham*, Cosmographical Glass *(1559), a title-page in constant use for different books till 1600. Note: 3 Ages of Man and the ancient authorities still retained.*

The flesh in each case is the same but, so to speak, differently employed. One suggests extensive and explorative verbal artistry while the other embodies the bone and sinew of thought and paraphrasable meaning. Our own Ordinary Level examinations demand the ability which once was attained at university but which was nevertheless introduced as the basis of a school curriculum.

Arithmetic, too, was taught at school and again completed at a much later period. Here, in a comic little chart by Robert Fludd (19), children were taught to salute the donkey: worthless at first but when raised to the power 10 quite elevated:

> like a cipher
> (Yet standing in rich place) I multiply . . .
> (*The Winter's Tale*, I. ii)

Then, as now, there was also a public for informative adult books in a simple idiom. One of these, chosen primarily for its attractive title-page (20), pleased a middle-class public who could buy paperback books for about the same proportionate cost as our own. However, this example, which was published more than a decade after the Copernican revolution, was completely outdated and unalterably Ptolemaic.

2 University: *Quadrivium*

Students at first completed the Trivium in the years from 15 or 16 when they reached either Oxford or Cambridge. There, with their B.A. degree after their names, they could proceed to further studies for the M.A.:

> MUSIC with tunes delights the ear
> And makes us think of heaven.
> ARITHMETIC by number can make
> Reckonings to be even.
> GEOMETRY things thick and broad
> Measures by line and square.
> ASTRONOMY by stars doth tell
> Of foul and eke of fair.

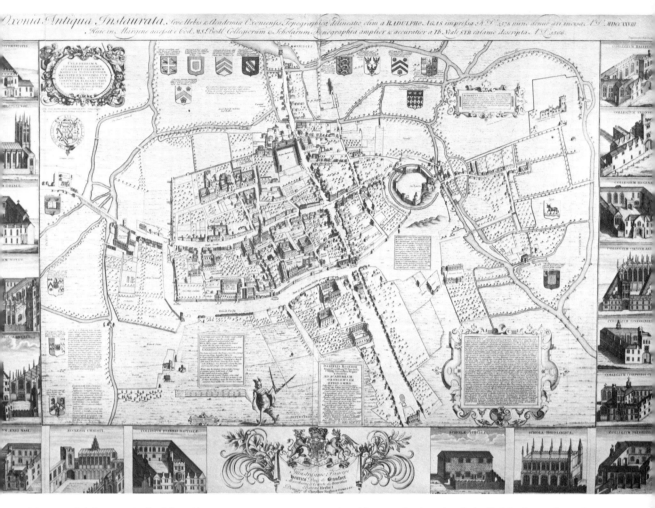

21a *Randulph Agas, Oxford (1578).*

Wilson's doggerel has certainly deteriorated but he has outlined the rest of the basic arts curriculum which we shall discuss on later pages. The Fine Arts, we see, were not Art in the Middle Ages.

With their numbers standing at about 2000 students apiece, sixteenth-century Oxford and Cambridge were still monastic, all-male preserves, tutored largely by bachelors, in whom a sense of remoteness was often retained in the cause of academic peace. Many College Fellows probably failed to see academic tradition as a *developing* body of knowledge, but many students may have only wanted their universities as guides for the future. Even so, the Elizabethan period saw the first attempts to teach English history and what we should now call English literature, while university

scientific work involved individuals rather than teams. If we believe Gabriel Harvey, writing to his friend the poet Edmund Spenser, the Cambridge of the 1570s was aflame with novelty. He instanced the study of Machiavelli, Petrarch and Boccaccio imported from Italy, and there was also the new dialectic of the Frenchman, Ramus. Much of this was quite aside from the standard curriculum in the university and represented the individual choices of the different colleges. Harvey added that Aristotle, Plato and Xenophon were being dethroned and regretted that 'subtle and effectual disputing' was on the decline. This was not an ossified or tradition-riddled university. It was also an education that attracted more and more gentry since illiterate boors and new country houses did not mix.

The historian William Harrison admired Oxford

for the 'woods on the hills aloft and goodly rivers in the bottoms and valleys' (21a) while Cambridge possessed more 'orderly compaction' in its make-up. The Oxford map leaves out of sight, as it must, the twisty, windy alleys and makes much of Christ Church (*Ecclesia Christi*), Wolsey's foundation, and other attractions by supplying marginal prints.

The Theology School (second square from the right) was to become the Bodleian Library in 1602, one of the greatest of all benefactions to the university as a whole.

The Cambridge picture (21b) highlights the academic buildings once more, since an academic icon exists to do just that. King's Chapel is shown

21b *Richard Lyne,*
Cambridge (1574).

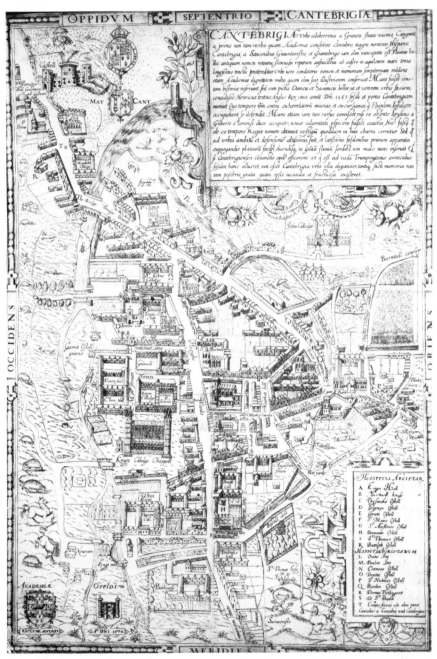

(inaccurately) in all its eminence, but there was space in 1574 for a few animals and boats to fill the empty areas of the town. Sidney Sussex College and Emmanuel College were founded too late for inclusion, though the latter as the Puritan stronghold was to be one of the most distinguished additions to the university at the end of the reign of Elizabeth and helped give it new qualities.

It is worth placing beside these two maps an acute diagnosis of the two educational centres by the modern writer, Patrick Cruttwell, in *The Shakespearean Moment*:

OXFORD	CAMBRIDGE
Royalist	Parliamentarian
Anglo-Catholic	Puritan
Medieval in theology	Scientific in philosophy
Optimist	Pessimist
Flamboyant	Austere.

As a symbol of a university student's career Dr John Caius of Gonville and Caius College, Cambridge (to be found near the inscription *Henney* in the map) fashioned a series of gates. Humility and Virtue were the first qualities he made into replicas of ancient arches, the latter showing Fame and Riches overhead. One is meant to ask: are riches the reward of Virtue or its pragmatic purpose? He then rounded off his visual conceit by the Gate of Honour (22), said to complete the first Renaissance building-scheme in England. Having stayed in the College for a course of four or seven years, with the Trivium and the Quadrivium mastered, the student was to walk out of this gate and collect his degree at a ceremony which would attest his intellectual energies and his suitability for a variety of personal and public offices and duties.

There was still time in a student's life to proceed to the doctorate and discover any number of other intellectual challenges. Dr John Dee, a noted Oxford scientist and mathematician, printed a mathematical *Groundplat* in 1570 in which he listed Perspective, Astronomy, Music, Cosmography, Astrology, Static, Anthropography, Trochlic, Helioscopy, Pneumatithmy, Menadry, Hypogeiody, Hydragogy, Horometry, Zography, Architecture, Navigation, Thaumaturgic and Archemastry (each with definitions) as suitable derivatives from a good mathematical education. Dee, however, was one of the great eccentrics: a scholar with a reputation in the fields of alchemy and spiritualism, a secret agent who used 007 as his personal emblem, as well as a distinguished navigator. His influence showed an independence that is the enemy of mental inertia. The author of the next work to be cited remained much more central to the intellectual tradition of the country.

22 *Caius College, Cambridge, Gate of Honour (1574). Tudor or Gothic decorations beneath, Ionic columns above: the earliest Renaissance style-medley in England.*

3 Creation Examined

Dr Helkiah Crooke labelled the title-page of his vast folio (23) in Greek because the idea of man as the microcosm, the world in little, originated in ancient philosophy. All the emblems he chose have their fascination, especially the Vein Man and the Pregnant Woman, two stereotypes of medical literature. Another contemporary work, J. Jonston's *A History of the Wonderful Things of Nature*,

23 *Helkiah Crooke,*
Microcosmographia
(1631). Legendary and scientific emblems, exceptional emphasis upon medical icons.

related the points of the compass to parts of man's body in a very definite way: 'Man hath the East in his mouth, the West in his Fundament, the South in his navel, the North in his back.' Since, according to popular Renaissance theory, men and

women are the mirrors of the planets and the spheres as well as their playthings, there existed a great deal of amateur speculation in astronomy that deserves quotation because it was immediately taken up into the rhetoric of play after play and poem after poem as aesthetically compulsive.

Peter Apian's *schema* of the Ptolemaic cosmos (24), though close upon the period of Copernicus, makes a most interesting comparison with Thomas Digges's later diagram below. Notice first the cluster of symbols in the centre: the two base elements (earth and water) and the two noble ones (fire and air). All of them are familiar, with the exception of the circle of fire said to surround the earth, the home of comets occasionally glimpsed behind the immediate sky. Air we believe to be a gaseous medium with a chemical formula. In the Middle Ages, however, it was

24 *Peter Apian,*
Cosmographia *(1539). Onion-like diagram with transparent spheres moving at different speeds round the earth, still ancient in allegiance.*

the medium through which the angels travelled and which was permeated with the grace of heaven. Scholars noticed that the entire cosmos moved from *east to west* while the individual spheres had the contrary motion from *west to east*, creating a tension between the individual planet and the macrocosm. In medieval thought, what was anti-clockwise to us was clockwise to God; all resulting friction was a derivative from human weakness. Planets indeed wished to be 'wandering stars' and in the process acted as a perfect poetic image for the clash between self-willed contains the cosmological gossip of the early Renaissance. It remained a best-seller for over a century and provided Spenser with the groundwork of his great pastoral poem, *The Shepherd's Calendar* (1579). It still provides the modern reader with the philosophical commonplaces of the past, moving from the discoveries of astronomy to the speculations of astrology without

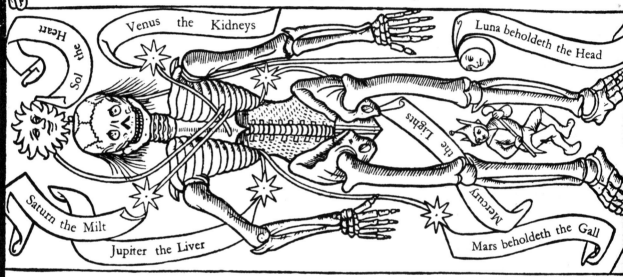

By this figure one may understand the parts of man's body over the which the planets hath might and domination to keep them from touching of any iron, nor to make incision of blood in the veins that proceedeth, in the time while that the planet of the said part is conjoined with any other planet malevolent, without having regard of some good planet that might encumber and let his evil course.

We may know by this figure the bones and joints and all the parts of the body as well within as without, of the head, neck, shoulders, arms, hands, sides, breast, back, haunches, thighs, knees, legs, and of the feet. The which bones shall be named and numbered hereafter, and it is called the Figure Anatomy.

temperament and the divine master-plan, as in Donne:

> Pleasure or business, so, our Souls admit
> For their first mover, and are whirled by it.
> Hence is't, that I am carried towards the West
> This day, when my Soul's form bends towards
>   the East.
>
> ('Good Friday, Riding Westward')

On the most distinctly popular level Guy Marchant's *Kalendar and Compost of Shepherds*

25 *Guy Marchant,* Kalendar and Compost of Shepherds *(1493).*
Man and planetary dominion.

hindrance or problem. From its pages any 'shepherd' could learn that the sun and moon were not alone in their visible effects on earth: each of the planets was bound by divine love and pressure to exert an influence upon those born under its aegis. Who could fail to be struck by the gruesome *memento mori* (25)? It taught that a

26 (right) *Guy Marchant,* Kalendar. *Man and zodiacal influence.*

27 (below) *Thomas Digges,* Perfect Description *(1576). Copernican model with sun in centre and not in the middle of planets, infinite space in place of the original divine sphere.*

person's good and ill days accorded with the planet and the sign of the zodiac with which he is saddled throughout life.

The text accompanying the illustration provided the popular opinions about the individual planets in the following manner:

SATURN: much theft and little charity, much lying and much lawing. And much plenty of corn and hogs.

MARS: stirreth men to bear weapons, as murderers, daggers, swords.

SUN: comforteth both man and beast, fish and all fowls.

VENUS: causeth joy among young folk; she reigneth on all men that be jealous and on women also.

MERCURY: very full and dry of nature, the lord of speech.

MOON: lady of moisture and ruleth the sea. Men born under the Moon shall be formed of body and have merry looks.

These notes resume a copious astrological literature that was familiar to doctors, alchemists and most other scientists. In the light of it, then, it was pointless for Romeo, the hero of a typical early Shakespearean tragedy, to protest: 'I defy you, stars.' This, as his fate showed, was immaturity and romantic nonsense.

It is possible to run the influence down to more intimate details, as John Maplet wrote in *Dial of Destiny* (1581):

In the head of man there are seven Pores or holes, allotted to diverse and sundry offices, as of the which every one of them is subject to a sundry Planet. As that Pore or hole which is in the right Ear appertaineth to Saturn; that in the left, to Jupiter. Mars also hath the government of that which is in the right side of the nose: Venus of the contrary: Sol is master over that which holdeth the strings of the right Eye: Luna over the other in the left Eye: and all the whole workmanship of the mouth is proper alone to Mercury.

For such a discovery we are our own models, subject in our own bodies to many unexpected influences (26).

To return now to Apian's *schema*: consider the outer rings of this onion. The eighth ring is the firmament, home of fixed stars; the ninth, *Cristallinum*, a slow-moving belt revolving once in 49,000 years where the signs of the zodiac are

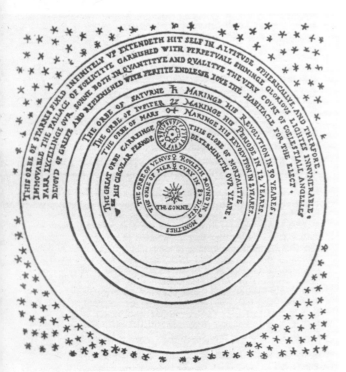

arranged (24). *Primum Mobile* (the tenth circle), the master-spring of the universe, is a metaphor of God the Father. There exist even more complex diagrams to which the nine orders of angels are added, each receding further and further from earth and always adding their glory to God whose centre was thought to be everywhere but whose circumference nowhere.

Thomas Digges, a distinguished follower of Copernicus, offered readers his own version of the Pole's theories with the *schema* (27). Immediately we notice that earth and sun have changed places and that the moon, shown in her epicycle, is reduced correctly to the status of a satellite. Yet the changes are by no means vast and Copernicus has been called a conservative revolutionary. In his thesis he imagined the fixed stars still confined within a sphere, but Digges for his part showed them occupying an infinity of space, a fact which Galileo in due course confirmed with the aid of his telescope.

No doubt every reader of seventeenth-century poetry is familiar with John Donne's dry reflections upon the effect of the new science upon religion and the old face of the universe:

> And new philosophy calls all in doubt,
> The element of Fire is quite put out;
> The Sun is lost, and th'earth, and no man's wit
> Can well direct him where to look for it.
>   ('The First Anniversarie')

We have to be on our guard: Donne was a student of Galileo, Kepler and Gilbert's magnetism, and it destroys him to make him a hopeless old conservative. In 'The Primrose', for instance, he made use of Galileo's findings on the Milky Way. Once thought to be a wash of vast cloud, the 'Galaxy' was freshly seen in 1610 to be a congregation of stars:

> their form and their infinity
> Make a terrestrial galaxy,
> As the small stars do in the sky.

Or, again, a sermon delivered in 1626 seems a lesson in geometry:

> The earth itself being round, every step we take upon it must necessarily be a segment, an arch of a circle. But yet though no piece of a circle be a straight line, yet if we take any piece, nay, if we

take the whole circle, there is no corner, no angle in any piece, in the entire circle. A perfect rectitude we cannot have in any ways in this world; in every calling there are some inevitable temptations.

The cosmology that attracted the Metaphysical poets was of no less compulsiveness for the most forward-looking painters. Otto Benesch, in his rewarding book, *The Art of the Northern Renaissance*, makes this clear in these words: 'The creative mind at a given historical moment thinks in certain forms which are the same in the arts and the sciences.' One great work Benesch cites is Pieter Brueghel's *Tower of Babel*, a legendary building made to appear as a cross between the Colosseum in Rome and the Leaning Tower of Pisa, slightly inclining yet reaching up and up into the clouds, level upon level, like the very rings of the universe, almost a metaphysical poem in oils.

The next diagram takes those all-embracing rings and shows once more man's place (28). It is a use of the male nude frequently used in philosophical drawings, sometimes called the 'Vitruvian man' and most familiar of all from Leonardo da Vinci's version and interpreted in these lines:

> By the lay [of the body] in his full length, and then spreading the arms and legs to their widest compass, they have contrived both the perfect square and exact circle: the Square by four right lines at four uttermost points of the hands and feet: the Circle by rounding a line about those points, placing the centre of their compass upon the navel.

Circles and squares thereafter imposed human proportions upon architecture. Pillars, for instance, have 'capitals' or heads, and identifications are pursued much further. Some columns were thought to be masculine, such as the Doric, while others were feminine, and a large building like a church to attain perfect balance in the eye of the unsuspecting beholder only when its mathematical ratios reflected those attained in the human body. A tall man, on this principle, needed a taller house, and what Dr John Dee called Anthropography came to the assistance of the architect who was determined to build well and proportionably to his client.

The element of humour in this cannot be denied and the best English poetic illustrations of such

28 (left) *Robert Fludd,* Utriusque Cosmi. *Title-page with 'Vitruvian man' in the midst of a universe of concentric circles.*

29 (right) *Guy Marchant,* Kalendar. *Choleric, Sanguine, Phlegmatic and Melancholic temperaments or complexions with animal emblems.*

Anthropography comes in a witty metaphysical poem, 'Upon Appleton House', by Andrew Marvell who at one point wonders how an obese owner can influence an edifice:

> But where he comes the swelling Hall
> Stirs, and the Square grows Spherical.

Appleton, like Palladio's Villa Rotonda (p. 10), was surmounted by a cupola and displayed the fruitful interpenetration of circle and square, the two forms whose relationship puzzled mathematicians for centuries. Marvell continues his Anthropography thus:

> Humility alone designs
> These short but admirable lines,
> By which, ungirt and unconstrained,
> Things great are in less contained.
> Let others vainly strive t'immure
> The Circle in the Quadrature.
> These holy Mathematicks can
> In every Figure equal Man.

4 The Humours and the Souls in Man

Behind the thighs of Fludd's microcosmos-man lie the four humours of which he himself is composed: choler, blood, phlegm and melancholy or black bile. In varying individuals the humours are differently balanced and in each person the constant pattern becomes his *complexion*. We may be accustomed to that word in a modern and debased sense in the context of the skin or the soap it takes to improve upon nature. In its correct denotation a human complexion is a complex, a tying together of a number of opposing forces resident in the body-fluids: the face is only a window to what lies within. We may read the following descriptions alongside (29) to gain some impression of the four stereotypes:

CHOLERIC MAN hath nature of FIRE, hot and dry, naturally is lean and slender, covetous, ireful, hasty, brainless, foolish, malicious. He hath wine of the LION: he chideth, fighteth and commonly he loveth to be clad in black.

SANGUINE MAN hath nature of AIR, hot and moist. He is large, plenteous, attempered, amiable, abundant in nature, merry, singing, laughing, liking, ruddy and gracious. He hath his wine of the APE: more he drinketh the merrier he is and draweth to women, and naturally loveth high coloured cloth.

PHLEGMATIC MAN hath nature of WATER, cold and moist. He is heavy, slow, sleepy, ingenious, commonly he spitteth when he is moved, and hath his wine of the SHEEP, for when he is drunken he accounteth himself wisest, and loveth most green colour.

MELANCHOLIC MAN hath nature of EARTH, cold and dry. He is heavy, covetous, backbiter, malicious and slow. His wine is of the HOG, for when he is drunken he desireth sleep. And he loveth black colour.

What is said there about the beasts in man come from a psychology of drink illustrated in other books: with alcohol inside him a man is least inhibited and possibly most himself and truest to his nature. Della Porta (30), the founder of Physiognomy, stood firmly upon the idea that body and soul, being inseparable, as Aristotle taught, the inner nature will inevitably come to view. He further believed that the complexion and inner passion would through time condition the outer appearance, or that physiology would indeed surface in the physiognomy. In such a way, also, voices were classified and when individual features were compared with those of an animal or bird the way lay open for a sustained metaphor in poetry. Similarly the theory of the humours itself proved highly suggestive to Ben Jonson writing the twin plays, *Every Man In His Humour* and *Every Man Out Of His Humour*, where the dramatist's idea was the Aristotelean one that humour and complexion 'may by metaphor apply unto the whole disposition'.

The theologian ought to be left to determine whether the invisible forces of the soul made

30 *G. della Porta,*
Fisonomia *(1623).*
(a) *Bull: Choler and
belligerence befitting a
Tamburlaine invest the
man.*

(b) *Wolf: Short neck denotes
cunning, and open mouth,
ignorance. Though intended
scientifically these could
be the origin of modern
cartoons.*

the body waste away or whether, on the other hand, it was the bodily disposition that ruined the soul's chances in the after-life. Galen, one of the early medical authorities, abdicated from the problem, saying: ''tis hard to decide which of the two do most harm to the other.' However, as a means to 'know thyself' (*nosce teipsum*, a favourite dictum) the categorization of the humours was highly esteemed, though not accepted as unchangeable from birth. Table A contrives to suggest that the prevailing wind might even have its effect!

Humour	Planet	Sign	Element	Wind	Season	Age
SANGUINE In Liver	Jupiter	Gemini Libra Aquarius	Air	*Auster* (South)	Spring	Childhood
CHOLERIC in Yellow Bile	Mars	Aries Leo Sagittarius	Fire	*Favonius* (West)	Summer	Adolescence
PHLEGMATIC from Blood	Moon	Taurus Virgo Capricorn	Water	*Eurus* (East)	Autumn	Manhood
MELANCHOLY in Spleen	Saturn	Cancer Scorpio Pisces	Earth	*Aquilo* (North)	Winter	Old Age

Table A: The Four Humours, *Adapted from R. Walkington's* Optic Glass *(1631).*

31 *C. Bovillus* Liber de
Sapiente *(1509). Four
Grades of Man. In this
most important diagram
the scholar is naturally
awarded the prize.*

Complete unanimity prevails over the interpretation of the essential plate (31). Its stepwise
pattern makes it immediately comprehensible.
Petra has only existence where *Arbor* adds life.
Equus as a noble animal combines all the fore-
going and is capable of movement and the operation of the senses. The chart is perhaps too simple:
other writers pressed the claims of eagles and

dolphins in their own natural elements just as
the alchemists erected a scale of metals with gold
at the head. *Homo* alone possesses 'discourse of
reason' though not every unacademic reader
would have agreed with the primacy of the
scholar among men. Others are shown to slip
down the scale to the status termed by us *vegetable*
when it seems cosmographically to be *rock*. Men,

27

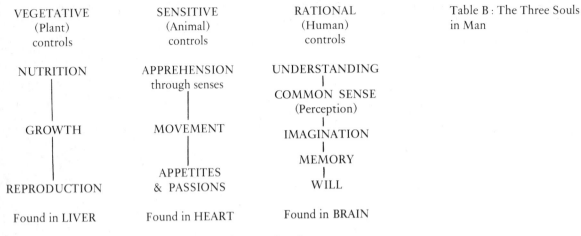

VEGETATIVE (Plant) controls	SENSITIVE (Animal) controls	RATIONAL (Human) controls	Table B: The Three Souls in Man
NUTRITION	APPREHENSION through senses	UNDERSTANDING	
		COMMON SENSE (Perception)	
GROWTH	MOVEMENT	IMAGINATION	
		MEMORY	
REPRODUCTION	APPETITES & PASSIONS	WILL	
Found in LIVER	Found in HEART	Found in BRAIN	

In judgment of her [soul's] substance thus they vary;
  And thus they vary in judgment of her seat;
For some her chair up to the *brain* do carry,
  Some thrust it down into the stomach's heat.
Some place it in the root of life, the *heart*
  Some in the *liver*, the fountain of the veins.
      John Davies, *The Soul of Man* (1599)

32 (facing page)
Albrecht Dürer,
Melencolia I (1517)
demonstrates intellectual
vitality and threatening
aspects of this humour.

in the full complexity of their make-up, recapitulate the characteristics of other creatures, subordinating them all to reason but accepting each as a valid archetype—see Table B in which these souls are detailed.

No reader of Elizabethan literature can progress far without finding reference to both physiology and physiognomy after these models. Our initial unfamiliarity can soon be dispelled and before long we find great pleasure in breathing its air. A single passage from *Hamlet*, an especially rich play, suffices: Hamlet here bitterly anatomizes his mother's conduct and her abdication of reason and fastidiousness in yielding to Claudius:

> Sense sure you have,
> Else could you not have motion, but sure that
>   sense
> Is apoplexed, for madness would not err,
> Nor sense to ecstasy* was ne'er so thralled
> But it reserved some quantity of choice
> To serve in such a difference. What devil was't
> That thus hath cozened † you at hoodman blind?
> Eyes without feeling, feeling without sight,
> Ears without hands or eyes, smelling sans all,
> or but a sickly part of one true sense
> Could not so mope.

* madness   † cheated

And understanding of so many abstract terms revives for us the pressure that Shakespeare knew he could gain from them. To redress the balance, take the characterization and the humours of Brutus, the chivalric man ('gentle') much admired by Shakespeare:

> His life was gentle, and the elements
> So mixed in him that Nature might stand up
> And say to all the world, 'This is a man.'

5 Melancholy Anatomized

One humour alone was always the scapegoat and made the subject of an individual literature. Timothy Bright's *Treatise of Melancholy* (1586) is still reprinted, but the masterpiece is Robert Burton's *Anatomy of Melancholy* (1621). An equally celebrated emblem is Dürer's subtle example (32) which Burton himself analysed. He immediately noted the duality of the picture. The woman has what he termed 'fixed looks, neglect habit, held therefore by some proud half-mad humour and yet of a deep reach [grasp], excellent apprehension [intelligence], judicious, wise and witty [creative].' His two distinct lines of thought may be presented in this fashion: Melancholy was held to be capable of deranging the mind as the facial expression and the emblem of the bat

tell us. Melancholy was equally a spur to speculative thinking and abstract reasoning as the tools discarded in meditation and the absorption of the features suggest. In addition, the angel in the picture and the rainbow were Dürer's way of reminding us that melancholy was not fatal. The keys of political power and the purse remain in sight to identify the high station to which melancholics might nevertheless be called. Had she been looking at a skull it would have been quite traditional and reminded us still more of Hamlet, who discusses dead Saturn-influenced types with his friends the Gravediggers.

The Elizabethans seemed to have been liberal and hospitable to all mixtures of temperament. Since nobody was responsible for the chain in which he was tied from birth why should they not? There were no words in the English language at that date to correspond to our 'sexually inhibited', 'compulsively active', 'acutely depressed' and the like: such terms seem inhuman and mechanistic. Nor did they have the word or the concept, often pleasant to us, 'normal' and 'normality'. They were not prepared, therefore, to pinpoint the norm but forecast the behaviour that might be expected from a man with a certain complexion and, provided that he lived well, they were tolerant. Melancholy was an interesting case in point. Because it was thought to be the fortune of intellectuals to be slave to it Jacobean England especially was overrun by pretended melancholics. Travellers from abroad were traditionally imbued with it. In *As You Like It* the melancholy Jaques, it will be remembered, is a traveller, and in the revenge tragedies of a later date there are many other examples. Bosola, in Webster's *The Duchess of Malfi*, provides another striking melancholic. Timothy Bright said of the whole type that it was subject to 'the fullest of variety of passion' and it seems that there has been no other humour so fruitful for the dramatist's casebook or one which yielded such excellent results. The Elizabethans, however, did not condemn the melancholics; they only asked for a moderate degree of social conscience, hoping that the experience of age would over-ride even the obsessiveness of this most passionate of humours. However, in later centuries it was always melancholy that attracted most attention from poets.

6 The Ages of Man

The same melancholy Jaques of *As You Like It* is made the mouthpiece of one of the all-connecting speeches in the play, and one which has been employed as an all-connecting Shakespearean theme, the famous:

> At first the *infant*,
> Mewling and puking in the nurse's arms.
> Then the whining *school-boy*, with his satchel
> And shining morning face, creeping like snail
> Unwillingly to school. And the *lover*
> Sighing like a furnace, with a woeful ballad
> Made to his mistress' eyebrow. Then a *soldier*
> Full of strange oaths, and bearded like the pard,
> Jealous in honour, sudden and quick in quarrel,
> Seeking the bubble reputation
> Even in the cannon's mouth. And then the *justice*
> In fair round belly with good capon lined,
> With eyes severe and beard of formal cut,
> Full of wise saws and modern instances;
> And so he plays his part. The sixth age shifts
> Into the lean and slippered *pantaloon* (33)
> With spectacles on nose and pouch on side,
> His youthful hose, well saved, a world too wide
> For his shrunk shank; and his big manly voice,
> Turning again toward childish treble, pipes
> And whistles in his sound. Last scene of all,
> That ends this strange eventful history,
> Is *second childishness* and mere oblivion,
> Sans teeth, sans eyes, sans taste, sans everything.

There is not an observation that has not become proverbial or an image that had not existed before the play. Experts continually discover literary sources for sententious statements in this passage and hunt out pictorial analogues for the entire sequence. We have already (p. 16) seen a Three Ages group. It is known that there was a Seven Ages tapestry at Hampton Court that Shakespeare may well have seen and there exists a composition of floor-tiles in Siena Cathedral which the poet may well not have been aware of. It must be insisted that as it stands in the play the 'world is a stage' speech is there to spotlight the speaker's disillusionment and little else.

Plate (34) showing the movement from Generation to Corruption over the top of a wheel is an outstanding example of pictorial analogue. The rim of the wheel proclaims: 'It is as water slipping away: they pass away. Furnished thus they are

33 (left) *Jacques Callot,* Pantalone, *original of Shylock and Marlowe's Barabas, two rich Pantaloons.*

34 (below) *Ages of Man, fifteenth-century illustration from* Archaeologia *(1853) relating Generatio (Birth) to Corruptio (Death).*

born into this life.' *Infans, Pueritia Adolescentia, Juventus, Virilitas, Senectus* and *Decrepitus,* adding up to 70 years, offer concrete embodiment of this 'strange eventful history' and open in the mind a whole vista of human experience. One single extract from *King Lear* similarly comprehends an inauspicious birth and a premature death, when Edmund and Edgar meet in Act V:

EDGAR: The dark and vicious place where he got
        Cost him his eyes   *Generatio* (34)
EDMUND: Thou hast spoken, 'tis true.
        The wheel has come full circle. *Corruptio* (34)

It may be ungracious to artists whose work has been quoted, men with an unshakable assurance in the divine plan, to suggest that at all costs they included everything so that in the end it signified a little less than it might. As one step towards a greater comprehensive picture, a configuration of positively everything in microcosm and macro-cosm, the reader is invited to consider Table C which shows the notion of correspondences far too hard at work.

7 Three Pictures of Religion

Had the subject of our discussions been works of medieval literature, it would have been necessary long before this time to give consideration to the Catholic religion as the central all-connecting thread. Yet, as the evidence above has shown, Man himself has become the all-absorbing issue and Christianity, though assumed and implicit, seems only to oil the wheels which are then left to spin over.

One immediately finds a further difficulty: there was not one sect in England about 1600, but three: Anglican, Puritan and Catholic, each of which must be given pictorial attention.

St Paul's Cross of 1620 (35) is an icon and a

	Planet	Signs	Element	Complexion	Virtues	Season	Stones	Colour	Day	Months	Flowers	Numbers	Metals
INFANCY	Moon	Scorpio Pisces	Water	Phlegmatic	Hope Innocency	Autumn	Marguerite Pearl	White	Monday	October November	Lily White Rose	10, 11	Silver
CHILDHOOD	Jupiter	Taurus Libra	Air	Sanguine	Justice Loyalty	Spring	Sapphire	Azure	Thursday	April September	Blue Lily	4, 9	Copper
ADOLESCENCE	Sun	Leo	Air	Sanguine	Faith Constancy	Spring	Topaz Chrysolith	Yellow	Sunday	July	Marigold	1, 2, 3	Gold
YOUTH	Venus	Gemini Virgo	Water	Phlegmatic	Loyalty in love Courtesy Affability	Spring	Emerald	Green Vert	Friday	May August	Green plants	6	Quicksilver
MANHOOD	Mars	Aries Cancer	Fire	Choleric	Charity Magnanimity	Summer	Carbuncle Ruby Coral	Vermillon Gules	Tuesday	March June July	Red rose Gillyflower	3, 10	Latten
GRAY HAIRS	Mercury	Sagittarus Pisces	Water Earth	Phlegmatic some Choleric	Temperance Prudence	Winter	Amethyst Opal Hyacinth	Purple	Wednesday	November February	Violet	7, 12	Tin
DECREPITUDE	Saturn	Capricornus Aquarius	Earth	Melancholy	Prudence Constancy	Winter	Diamond Agate Chelydonus	Black (Sable)	Saturday	December January	Aubifaine	5, 8	Iron Lead

Table C: Seven Ages
adapted from J. Ferne,
Blazon of Gentry *(1586).*

35 (facing page)
St Paul's Cross (1620)
with royal box beneath
Jehovah and small
distinguished congregation.
Both schema *of state*
church and icon *to be*
adored.

schema together. With Jehovah at the top, the King directly beneath and the leading ecclesiastical dignitaries present in the metropolitan cathedral, this was indeed an oil-painting with the old validity of a holy or votive picture. The birds in the sky may still—as in the Middle Ages —symbolize liberated souls; the men, women and animals in the foreground a cross-section of those still awaiting such freedom. Paul's Cross sermons were popular—far more than the select congregation would indicate—welcoming as many as 5000 people at a time for anything up to three hours. Had the picture been painted in the sixteenth century, and painted realistically, one might have seen people in white sheets doing penance. In 1586, for instance, a man charged with incitement to murder did penance and earned good marks for his addresses and edifying words 'against the frequented vice of usury' for good measure. At other times the congregation assembled for the excitement of official proclamations and contemporary news bulletins, making the scene a meeting-place of church and state, as the presence of King, Queen and Prince Charles here demands.

Equally and unexpectedly symbolic of the Anglican Church under Queen Elizabeth is the church of Woodham Walter in Essex (36). Built about 1563, still Gothic in style, for the Gothic never quite died out, it is as far as we know the

only church built in the country in the reign of Elizabeth. This is proof, if any were needed, of the poverty of the church whose clergy were both under-educated and under-paid, the majority of church-revenues feeding the pockets of local gentry rather than of the clerics themselves. As if their position were not precarious enough, the oldest of them, having seen the light before the Reformation, were theologically suspect. In effect, in spite of much theological scholarship among bishops, too many Elizabethan clergymen were no more than church-attendance officers whose task was to secure occasional conformity or propose a scale of fines.

Among the deviationists the most favoured in Elizabethan times were the Puritans—though their days of persecution lay ahead—and their intellectual leaders who spread out like a net from Cambridge may be symbolized in the figure of William Perkins (37) who is so little known today because a great deal of his work remained in Latin. Even so he was a popular man who attempted to codify the vague religious aspirations of the English followers of Calvin and Beza. He saw that the clergy could offer less spiritual consolation than their medieval forerunners.

HAGGAI CHAP: i VE: i 2? THVS SPEAKETH THE LORD OF HOSTS THIS PEOPLE SAIE, THE TYME IS NOT YET COME. THAT THE LORDS HOVSE SHOVLD BE BVILT 5 THEN CAME THE WORD OF THE LORD BY HAGGAI THE PROPHETT SAYING, IS IT TYME FOR YOV YOVRSELVES (O YEE) TO DWELL IN YOVR SEILED HOVSES & THIS HOVSE LYE WASTE:

IT IS WRITTEN; MY HOVSE IS THE HOVSE OF PRAYER; &c;

ST. PAUL'S CROSS.

An accurate delineation the only Correct Veiwe that remains of this Ancient and Curious Object as it appeared on Sunday the 26th of March, 1620, at which time it was visited by King James the I, His Queen and Charles Prince of Wales, attended by the Archbishop of Canterbury, Bishops, Officers of State, Nobility, Ladies &c &c. Who were received with great Magnificence by Sir William Cockaine Lord Mayor of London, assisted by the Court of Aldermen, Recorder &c, When a most excellent Sermon was preach'd from a text purposely selected by his Majesty (Psalm CII, Verse 13, 14,) by Dr John King Bishop of London, recommending the speedy reparation of the Venerable Cathedral of St Paul, which, with its unsteepled Tower, and incumberance of Houses &c, appear on the back, and side grounds.

This Print is Engraved from an Original Picture, in the possession of the Society of Antiquaries, London.

London, Published June 4, 1816 by R & Wilkinson, Nº 58 Cornhill.

36 *Woodham Walter,*
Essex. Parish church
(1563). Unremarkable in
Late Gothic style with
Flemish step-gables, but
symbolic as the only church
erected in Elizabeth's time
—and by the family of
Earl of Essex.

37 *The Face of Puritanism*
I: William Perkins (1558–
1602), most admired
Puritan academic
theologian (from T. Fuller,
The Holy State (1648);
('painfull' means
'painstaking').

WILLIAM PERKINS *The Learned, pious, and painfull*
Preacher of Gods word, at S.t Andrewes in Cambridge where
He died Anno Dñi. 1602. Aged 44 yeares.
W.M. Sculp:

Where Chaucer's Poor Parson heard confession, celebrated mass and offered communion, as well as presiding at ceremonies like church ales and occasional plays, the Puritans were restricted to their sermons and declarations so that lay-folk were, in effect, left to their own spiritual devices. This forced isolation lies behind such a book as *Pilgrim's Progress* or *Robinson Crusoe* and cannot be under-estimated. It followed logically from the reform of the Reformation that took place in Geneva and it is a total mistake to confuse academic Puritans like Perkins with the statue-breakers and the knaves and fools in Ben Jonson.

Perkins was drawn into the discussion of the business allegiance of members of his creed. The Elizabethan churches were unhappily in no position to emulate the welfare work of the medieval monasteries and convents when the Puritans announced the convenient doctrine that the poor were naturally unthrifty anyway and unfavoured by God. Similarly, it emerged, the rich and the thrifty were successful because of divine consent. All his ideas stem from the indispensable Calvinist idea of Justification by Faith alone and the decree of Predestination, which dismissed the majority of mankind to eternal flames. In his later days, it seems that Perkins became more encouraging and exhorted his congregations to try harder so that they might not go unrewarded.

Perkins provided a fine large chart demonstrating the operation of Salvation and Damnation which newly appears in H. C. Porter, *Puritanism in Tudor England*. I have therefore reprinted one by Théodore Beza, one of the leading Genevan theologians, which is a paradigm of the Calvinist way of the world (38). A précis is appended (see page 37), through which we can learn the groundwork of an unattractive but significant strand in English thinking.

The Christian is exhorted to study this visual aid in his religious education and ask himself 'Am I going to Heaven or Hell?'

Finally, the religious group which was more numerous than is usually assumed. About 1570, Catholics still outnumbered the Protestants and most of them remained loyal to Elizabeth, resenting the imputation that they were not. After 1574, however, when the Pope began to send foreign seminary priests and Jesuits into the country, the position was rendered too complex for unassuming Catholics. The fines for non-attendance at church (Recusancy) were stepped up and when the Jesuits began to stir disaffection against the Queen her 'final solution' (39) was reached. Religious freedom was forfeit until the end of her reign and the number of martyrs created was large and almost at variance with the nature of a tolerant state that had yet felt the blow of a religious war.

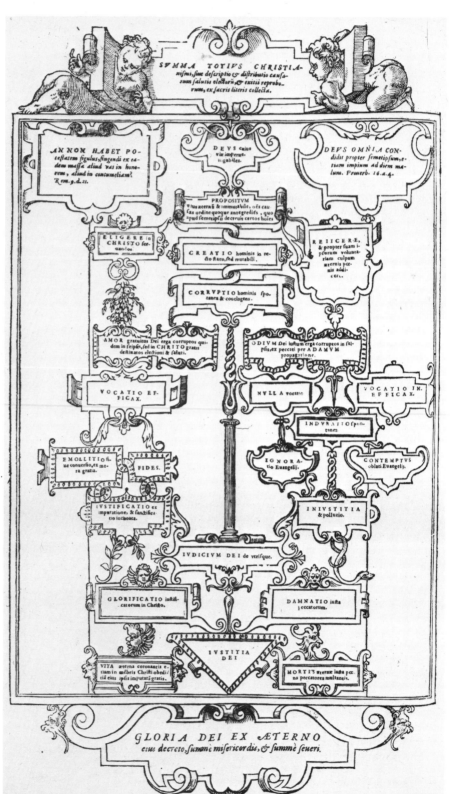

38 *Théodore Beza,*
Tractation *(1582). Map
of a Calvinist's Progress.
Notice the decorative motifs .
For précis see facing page.*

SUMMARY OF ALL CHRISTIAN DOCTRINE
showing the pattern of salvation
and reprobation out of the Gospels

GOD IS INSCRUTABLE IN HIS WAYS
Both decreed and proposed to man

ELECTION
in Christ

REJECTION
through Sin

The Creation of Man whose
Corruption is voluntary
but inevitable

GRACIOUS LOVE
through Christ
towards men
corrupt in
essence

JUST HATRED
by God for
Adam's sin
spreading
corruption

EFFECTUAL VOCATION

INEFFECTUAL VOCATION

FAITH

CONVERSION
Justification through
Christ's imputed righteousness

IGNORANCE AND CONTEMPT
OF THE GOSPEL
Rebelling against Justice

DIVINE IMPARTIAL JUDGEMENTS

GLORIFICATION

CONDEMNATION

ETERNAL LIFE

DIVINE JUSTICE

ETERNAL DEATH

ETERNAL GLORY TO GOD
FOR ALL HIS DEGREES

39 *Richard Verstegan,*
Theatrum Crudelitatum
*(1602). Note. (A) rack in
action and (D) cell
'litelease'. Compare 106.*

3. Stage by Stage

At this point we must turn to some of the physical elements, the brick, lath and plaster, the seats, pillars and platforms that make up the actors' workshop. A study of theatrical history embraces in turn all the arts and takes the student into history, geography, economics and construction-technology as well as into the minds of both writers and executants. Here we take a look at some of the illustrations that remain to us in an attempt to understand the problems of the theatrical community and the spectacles they prepared for their growing audiences.

In the 1570s there were three theatrical proto-types still at work in England. The first of these was soon abandoned: by the outbreak of the Civil War in 1642 the rest had followed suit. Yet, with profound adaptations, they sprang back to life and, in the hands of amateurs at least, all three are still likely to emerge at any time today in spite of a popular culture that has little use for them.

I. The scaffold stage, anchored to one outdoor location, as in (40) or else adapted to horse-and-cart and driven from station to station, was the home of the *Mystery Play*. As an essentially Catholic form, developing out of portions of church liturgy, it was the first to yield to the Reformation, remaining active only in a country like Spain. However, in England it left its traces behind. It was not necessary for a later dramatist to be a Catholic to perceive a mythological quality in the salvation of Isaac from the hands of Abraham or the destruction of the Holy Innocents at those of Herod. *Macbeth* shows Shakespeare's appreciation of the emotional force in both sequences: the

fortunate escape of Fleance to found the dynasty that led to James I, and the fate of Macduff's family of 'pretty ones'. To such scenes the books and plays from the Bible add their own emotional resonance.

Today we know little of the acting style used in these Mystery Plays. St Sebastian (41) as here portrayed breathes an impersonality in spite of immense pain which excites the spectator's own emotion. This may be the ideal towards which medieval actors aspired.

II. The indoor acting area—it is not a platform— cleared in feudal banqueting halls lasted into the era of the professional playhouse. For short after-dinner plays, known as *Interludes*, actors entered through curtains or wooden screens which divided the kitchen and service-area from the hall itself

40 (below left) *Thomas Sharp*, Dramatic Mysteries *(1825).* *Coventry Mystery Play.*

41 (right) *A. Pollaiuolo,* St Sebastian *(c. 1475).* *Modelled on a crucifixion with saint's response better depicted than the perspective.*

and took over a space in front of a high table. Any medieval dining hall, as in Oxford and Cambridge colleges, can give the same effect today. In (42) the strolling players, with their all-male personnel and conviviality, seem better equipped to give comic interludes, such as those written by John Heywood in the reign of Henry VIII, than the more serious ones known as the *Moralities* which re-enact the old fight of sin and salvation, order and disorder, and were adapted for performance both indoors and out. These in turn left their impression upon virtually all serious writers of drama and masque in Elizabethan and Stuart times who saw their works as moral microcosms.

The screen of the Hall of the Middle Temple (43) is one of the most ornately worked examples.

It reminds us that this hall witnessed the indoor first performance of *Twelfth Night*. Not far away, at Gray's Inn in 1594, another prominent court audience assembled for a less important entertainment, *Gesta Grayorum*, which nevertheless has its place in history. For such a performance, with Elizabeth herself present, the old order was inverted. The actors had the dais of the high table at last, a natural development towards the structure of a permanent theatre, while the audience entering at the screens end, and raised in the modern manner, found themselves looking at both the stage and Elizabeth herself isolated on a small platform in the centre of the hall.

III. The humblest of these prototypes, first identified in about 1200 in their costumes and their

outdoor acting circle on village greens, has the longest history of all. *Mummer's Plays*, usually representing a contest between an English warrior and a wild man or a foreigner, were bound by convention as much as a Punch-and-Judy show. In the course of the play the hero must be

43 *London, Middle Temple Hall. Elizabethan screen, Doric columns and hammerbeam roof form setting for original performance of* Twelfth Night.

44 (far left) *Pieter Brueghel,* Valentine and Orson *(1566). Valentine is a monarch; Orson, the wild man; while Bellisant holds ring for recognition and others go round with the hat.*

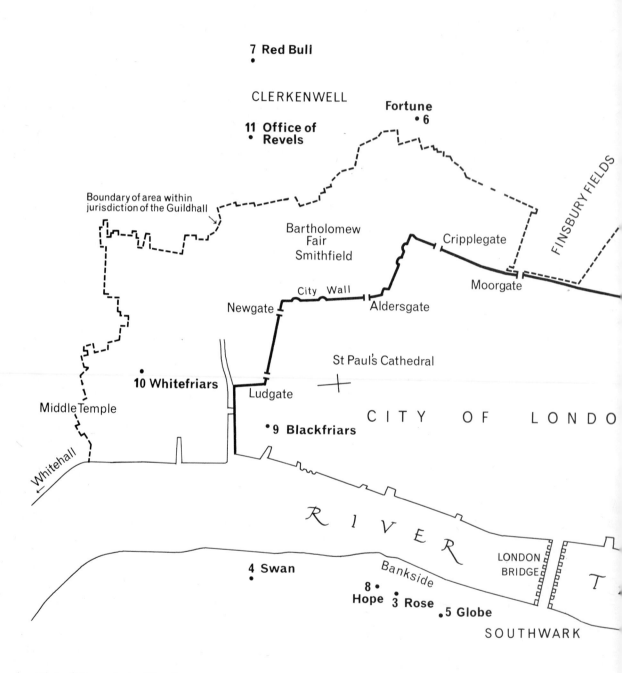

7 Red Bull

CLERKENWELL

Fortune
• 6

11 Office of
• Revels

Boundary of area within
jurisdiction of the Guildhall

Bartholomew
Fair
Smithfield

Cripplegate

FINSBURY FIELDS

Moorgate

City Wall

Newgate

Aldersgate

St Paul's Cathedral

10 Whitefriars

Ludgate

Middle Temple

•9 Blackfriars

CITY OF LONDO

Whitehall

R I V E R

LONDON
BRIDGE

T

4 Swan

Bankside

8 •
Hope 3 Rose
•5 Globe

SOUTHWARK

Chief London Playhouses

DATES

1 *(1576–97)*

2 *(1576 onwards) used for prizefights in 1620s*

3 *(c. 1587 onwards) used for prizefights in 1620s. Either this or (6) was partly modelled on a Tennis Court*

4 *(1595 to 1630s)*

5 *(1598) burnt 1613; rebuilt 1614; destroyed 1644*

6 *(1600) burnt 1621; rebuilt 1623; dismantled 1649*

7 *(1606) continued sporadically till 1663*

8 *Used for plays from 1614; destroyed after return to use as lion-den and bear-baiting in 1656*

9 *Notably used for plays: I 1576–84; II 1609–42. (Indoor, winter house) in Playhouse Yard*

10 *Used for plays in 1590s. (Indoor, winter house).*

11 *Warehouse for costumes, properties for use in theatres and centre of official control*

There was a Cockpit in Drury Lane (1616 onwards) and the Cockpit-in-Court, along with Banqueting House and Masque theatre at Whitehall off the map to the left.

Shoreditch
1 Theatre
2 Curtain

opsgate

City Wall

Aldgate

THE TOWER

M E S

wounded, cured and put on his feet again since anthropologists tell us that the entire contest (or *agon*) derives from primitive combats of Summer and Winter. Brueghel, always uncannily apt for our purposes, shows a Flemish folk-play (44) with a Wild Man named Orson whose colleagues might have been seen in the streets of London at the Lord Mayor's Show and may well have inspired Caliban in *The Tempest*. Again, in his painting *Procession to Calvary* a small circle is shown, with people banked all about waiting for the grisly ceremony. Outdoor circles of this type are still observable in Cornwall and there is one described for the first time in 1970 which is located at Walsham-le-Willows, Suffolk. These Game Places once were theatres in the round.

A nineteenth-century version of the Mummer's Play is described in Thomas Hardy's *Return of the Native*, a novel where the primitive world of Wessex seems naturally to throw up this old derivative. Experts can tell us of the survival of the traditional battle play, and at Marshfield in Gloucestershire, wild men dressed in strips of old newspaper still perform each year.

1 Summer Theatres and Winter Theatres

When that ambitious carpenter, James Burbage, built the first public playhouse in London at Shoreditch in 1576 he called it The Theatre from the Greek 'place for seeing' and had particularly in mind such open-topped arenas, circular and polygonal, as the bear-baiting and bull-rings which were in turn affected by his new form of entertainment. He had to adapt the necessary carpentry to the task, to form an acceptable gild or brotherhood with rules for partnership, workmanship and apprenticeship. He sought out patronage and had to keep on the right side of the authorities, though they were relatively harmless since Shoreditch was outside the London Magistrates' jurisdiction.

Unlike later and more aristocratic theatre-builders Burbage had no links with Italian precedent, but he may have known the open-air Rhetoric Theatres of Antwerp (45) and elsewhere in the Netherlands, a country with which many trade-connections were maintained and where learned plays were entered for academic trophies called *land-jewels*. In the end James, with his sons

Richard and Cuthbert, formed a company and a playhouse about which little is known. After 21 years, the lease having expired, he moved it to the opposite bank and opened it afresh as the Globe. The early playhouse document, the best that we have and one from which we depart at our peril, is of the Thames-side Swan Theatre which was in position some years before the Globe. The Utrecht traveller, De Witt, made this famous drawing (46), which leaves several points undecided. If it is a performance in progress on the stage and not a rehearsal, why is the prologue trumpeter still at his post? Are they musicians at the six windows or members of the audience? Why is no inner-stage structure shown or no hangings sketched in? What is shown is an open platform and the frontal of the *tiring house* (*mimorum aedes*) where the actors changed and collected for their entries, the completed metamorphosis of a Hall Screen with two inset double-doors for entries, and little else. The word *orchestra* (from the Greek theatre) is applied to the seats nearest the platform and the

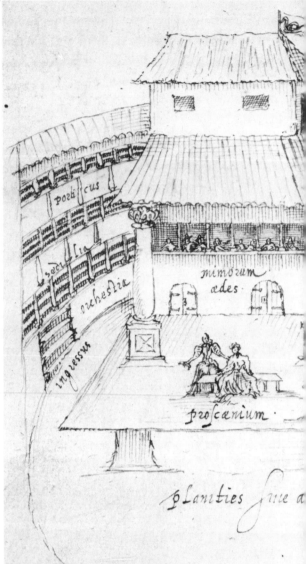

45 (left) *Antwerp, Rhetoric stage (Rederijker) crowned with city arms (1561). Compare* 118.

important Latin *proscenium* for the entire platform.

Modern investigators have insisted that the proscenium could not always have been so bare: it was not intended that plays show man completely divorced from the rest of creation, he was not always alone. Hangings showing sun, moon and stars as well as drapes in white, red and black (as used in *Tamburlaine*) were required. A scrutiny

tectum

46 *J. de Witt*, Swan Theatre *(1596) 'built of a mass of flint stones and supported by wooden columns painted in such excellent imitation of marble'.*

capacity to both the Swan and the Globe. He found that all agree at a width of about 48 feet. He has also made a model for the Swan based on De Witt, which shows it as a 24-sided polygon and not a circle, with a diameter of about 90 feet. Finally, Glynne Wickham has taken a step towards disposing of the legend that the New Inn, Gloucester, was one of the inspirations of London playhouse-building. By trying to produce a play there himself he found the snag: an inn yard was just too busy, and he abandoned the production. Strolling players used inns before there were theatres, but Professor Wickham is convinced that they kept to the indoor pattern of a hall stage. We have, therefore, no picture from Gloucester, picturesque though its courtyard is.

No authentic views are available of Burbage's second or third houses. The Globe can be identified without difficulty on Visscher's Long View (15) but other contemporary maps give it a different external appearance. Blackfriars Theatre, roofed and best suited for winter-time plays, was part of an old monastery already associated with boy players for almost a century when Burbage leased it. It must be admitted that there is no shortage of documentation referring to these and other playhouses and a number of scale models exist. The student is referred to Irvin Smith's two books on the Globe and the Blackfriars for a great deal of fact and conjecture, and to Bernard Beckerman's *Shakespeare at the Globe*, a most helpful study of one dramatist's work for this most celebrated stage.

Blackfriars Theatre charged a basic sixpence as admission as opposed to the penny entrance of the public playhouses. From 1576 there had been the troupe of boys in residence who are the subject of the famous piece of theatrical criticism in *Hamlet*:

HAMLET: Do the boys carry it away?
ROSENCRANTZ: Ay, that they do, my lord—Hercules and his load too.

The joke was that Hercules and his load were the outdoor emblem of the Globe and the boys had obviously been stealing their audiences. Boy actors at all times were entrusted with the female roles—except for a single and mysterious foreign troupe that brought women once in 1629 to the

of stage-directions has shown, on the other hand, that no permanent curtained inner stage was needed for a bedroom, a study or a cave, since any of these could be carried on and removed without being a fixture. These seem to be the most important facts that De Witt imparts. However, some scholars have gone a little further and still use De Witt's drawing with the greatest respect. Richard Hosley, for instance, has measured the Hall Screen at Middle Temple and that at Hampton Court and compared them with the tiring-house frontage of the Fortune Theatre, similar in

Blackfriars—and had achieved an expertise that dramatists respected. The boys themselves may well have seen themselves as circus animals at the whim of a trainer:

> He plucketh us by the nose, he plucketh us by
> the hawse,   [neck]
> He plucketh us by the ears with his most unhappy
> paws.

yet they were money-spinners.

Blackfriars, though called 'private', was not closed to anybody with sixpence. It gave better accommodation, better staging to look at and more music, and it was, unlike the public houses, roofed. It might more usefully be called a winter playhouse since it was most used at that season and known as "the torchy Friars" because of its visual effects. The truly exclusive theatre was that of the court with scene-changing devices, cloud-machines and the pictorial researches and architectural studies of Inigo Jones to recommend it. Italian models were consulted by him in the process of building a royal theatre and this fact, among others, distinguishes it completely from Globe and Blackfriars alike.

2 Academic and Court Theatres

The first prominent theatre-architect of the Renaissance, Serlio (1475–1554), recommended different sets for comedy and tragedy. He implanted on the stage some of the spectacle that was available to the painter of townscapes in full command of the art of perspective. This Leonardo da Vinci defined as 'nothing else than seeing a place behind a pane of glass'. For the Serlian comic set (47a) the painted backcloth and the cut-outs that formed the façades of houses on the stage had to show an inn, a church and a brothel, as here with Signora *Rufia*. For the tragic counterpart (47b) Serlio wanted everything more noble, colourful, expensive and courtly, since he recognized tragedy as an aristocratic art. To look at his sets is to be reminded of fifteenth-century paintings or, more properly, to see what it was in them that influenced the theatrical profession in Italy and elsewhere. The painting by Antonello (48) develops every imaginable viewpoint and renders the saint's unwontedly luxurious home into a potential stage. From it we understand a possible derivation of the spectacle theatre out of pictorial art.

47 a and b *Sebastiano Serlio,*
Comic and Tragic Scenes from
First Book of Architecture
(1611). A woodland scene
for satyr play also exists.

The most famous theatre-architect from
Vicenza was the great Palladio (1508–80), whose
churches and villas have been called the most imi-
tated buildings in history. His Teatro Olimpico
with its permanent set, originally built for a performance of *Oedipus* (50), sums up the past and
forecasts a theatrical future. Three thousand spec-
tators, roughly the number for the large London
playhouses, were to be accommodated on thirteen
semicircular stepped-up rows beneath a painted
sky and surrounded with classical statuary. On the
opening night in 1585, the tragedy was launched
with both music and perfume and a major theatre
was given to Europe. Since Palladio had not lived
to see the completion it was left to his pupil Sca-
mozzi to design the buildings on the sloping platform which to the present day give a perspective
of Thebes to the audience. Inigo Jones went to
Vicenza more than once when planning a similar
model for Whitehall and if one follows in his path

one sees the truth in the charge that the Renaissance theatre-builder was more obsessed with the
ancient past than with the future. Palladio's practical work had been based upon the circle-haunted
Vitruvius, the Roman architect, who failed to fore-
see that seventeenth-century and later Italian taste
would be principally operatic and that this posed
problems for housing and spacing that the most
capacious and symbolic circles would not solve.

There is a smaller Olimpico in an imperfectly
restored state at Sabbioneta, built in 1588 for the
Duke of Mantua, and a large rebuilt Teatro Farnese
(1618–19) at Parma, both open to the public. In
the latter, especially, the truth seems to have
dawned. At a time when there existed the operas
of Monteverdi, Cavalli and others, what was
needed was the prototype of an opera-house with
its horse-shoe and not the semicircle. Here too we
put a finger on the shortcoming of Italian theatre:
there is so little in the way of spoken drama and
only the 'low' *commedia dell'arte* seems to have
sprung from it. In these improvised comedies
lovers are rivalled by old fools (49) and hindered
by idiot servants (*zanni*) while for dialogue all that
was provided was a *scenario* and the effect was

48 (left) *Antonello*, St
Jerome *(c. 1460)*. *Fusion
of Italian perspectives with
Flemish details. Hugh
Casson has called it a perfect
example of Inscape.*

49 (above) *Pantalone
(seventeenth century
print). Simultaneous
picture in townscape
showing a Pantaloon and
a Captain in love.*

50 (right) *Vicenza, Teatro
Olimpico (1580)
Proscenium with five
entries and Hercules'
labours in topmost niches.*

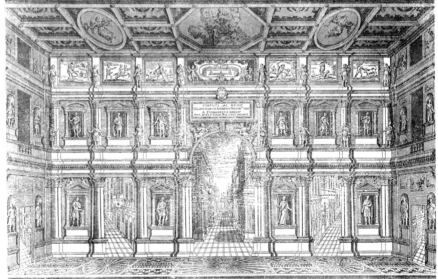

completely predictable. If it spilled over into
Shakespeare and is known to many millions today
in the characteristic roles always taken by the Marx

Brothers earlier in the present century in films, it
will be admitted that the voice of *commedia dell'-
arte* is still familiar.

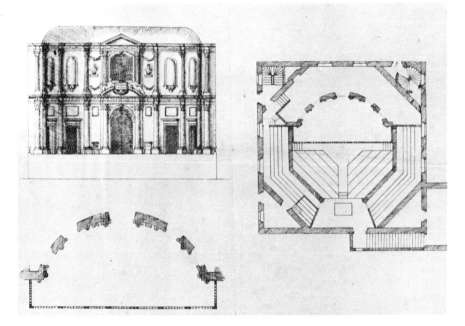

51 *Whitehall, Cockpit-in-Court Theatre (1630) by Inigo Jones. Modelled on 50, already out of date. Plaque reads 'Profit and Delight'.*

52 (below) *John Bulwer,* Chironomia *(1644). Stylized gestures for orator.*

By the time that Inigo Jones delivered his design for a five-entry stage, a concave scene and an octagonal auditorium (51) to be called the Cockpit-in-Court, he was fifty years out of date and all he could do was to add the latest scenic devices and machinery. By 1630 the vitality had gone out of the English dramatic renaissance and attempts to draw dramatists towards court-theatres and away from public-theatres succeeded no more in England than they had done in Italy. The possession of wealth and patronage alone could not command talent so that when the Civil War closed the theatres in 1642 it was hardly a year too soon.

3 Acting

Most serious of all in 1642 was the dropping of a tradition of acting which could not be recaptured in 1660. Even where a tradition is unbroken it develops. In the present century tragic acting has changed from a rhetorical, poetic manner to a naturalistic one, whereas comic acting has remained more stable. For mementoes of the Elizabethan style the best that can be found is the polyfoto-type print (52), where the formalized movement was apparently made to forecast the arrival of an emotion, or we can look for literary recollection in the text of a play.

The oratorical gestures which are so amusing to study were not systematized in book form till 1644, when there were no actors any longer in training. Lawyers and politicians were the main market for Bulwer's book and one may suppose that actors followed the practice of the legal profession, which was usually so alien to them. It is, however, a type of practice well in line with Elizabethan psychology in general. Even in the middle of the eighteenth century when the leading actor was David Garrick, it was said that 'the passions in all their operations were his constant study: their turns and counterturns, their flux and reflux.' Much the same might have been said of Richard Burbage, for a contemporary psychologist, Father Thomas Wright, in his *Passions of the Mind*, explained that passions (the word preferred for emotions) were physical forces inside the system capable of blinding judgement and seducing the will quite literally. Further, all passions were the same from one man to the next: one man's rage, lust or melancholy came from the same store as his neighbour's: the actor's task, therefore, was to be a representative of both of them and of all of us.

under the word *blood* by Shakespeare, as well as sorrow, regret and disillusionment to portray. His professional study was to build up a role from the conflicts of passions and their counterparts exactly as directed by the abstract words and their metaphors in the verse. To do this demands sensitivity and intelligence far beyond the boundaries of purveying entertainment.

When the play no longer drew the spectator the actor was ready to reach a man who was not originally considered by the dramatist, a reader. Occasionally, an enterprising printer would try to gain illegal possession of a popular play for a small *quarto* or pocketbook production, but he was usually obliged to wait until he was himself approached. The large *folio* format was extremely rare and was generally too expensive for plays. Since the most important dramatic manuscripts have disappeared we are infinitely grateful to the early printers (53). A craftsman like the blind William Jaggard whose firm undertook the Shakespeare First Folio deserves recognition as an essential link that binds the author, the playhouse company and printer of the text to us at the present day.

53 Elizabethan hand press as found principally in St Paul's Churchyard.

When Aristotle explained his view of *catharsis*, that human emotions were purged by drama, and when Vitruvius saw to it that theatres should be ventilated to allow the vapours thus purged to blow away at the end of a performance, they both saw the acting profession as a species of amateur psychiatrist. The Shakespearean interpreter has the passions of love, revenge and jealousy, all grouped

4. Emblems and Myths

Portrait painters apart, Elizabethan and Jacobean artists have little to offer to European art collections. Where indeed are English sculptures for open spaces comparable with those for which Italy is celebrated? The losses that we have sustained because of the absence of pictorial documentation, quite apart from the aesthetic considerations involved, are immense and incalculable but cannot be lamented for ever. We accept that Elizabethan art produced no images of cloudscapes, mountains or rainbows and must rest content with much less as a result.

One Italian miniature art form that suited English talents was the *Emblem*, a woodcut with a motto above and occasionally a poem below. It was familiar as a pattern for needlework or for tapestry, but it was never unexpected or exploratory in any way; always conservative in that it repeated a known moral. Panofsky has defined emblems as images which refuse 'to be accepted as representations of mere things but demand to be interpreted as vehicles of concepts.' Several such pieces occur in later pages for their utilitarian value in helping us to understand the working of the allegorical temper, and this fact alone will cause the reader to be wary. It was an art form beloved of the Puritan because an art so didactically desirable could hardly cause human errors. Yet, we may think, did so much moral art ladled out improve morale at all? We cannot stop for an answer.

The reader may study a large cluster of emblems that once decorated a room (54). Numbers 1–20 are not given but here are translations of texts that fitted into the empty bands. Some, it will be admitted, remain obscure but all have their fascination:

21 *Arsit, crepuit, evanuit:* Burning, crackling, vanishing.
22 *Et occulte, et aperte:* Both secretly and openly.
23 *Obscure, secure:* Safe through being hidden.
24 *Fronti nulla fides:* No trustiness to be found on his brow.
25 *Sat iniussa calet:* It glows sufficiently by itself.
26 *Ut moreris vives:* When you die you shall live.
27 *Trahit sua quemque:* Everyone is drawn by his own pleasures.
28 *O puzzi, o ponga:* Each calls the other foul-smelling.
29 *Spem fronte:* Hope on her brow is shown.
30 *Descendente adimpleor:* I fill up by going down.
31 *Pie sed temere:* Dutiful but rash.
32 *Iam sumus ergo pares:* Now we are alike in colour.
33 *Speravi et perii:* I was full of hope but caught fast.
34 *Pascor, at haud tutus:* Supping with danger.
35 *Odi profanum vulgus:* I loathe the common herd.
36 *Nusquam tuta fides:* Confidence is nowhere secure.
37 *Nec habet victoria laudem:* Victory gathers no praise.
38 *Mihi plaudo ipse domi:* Praise begins at home.
39 *Desipui sapiendo:* 'Tis folly to be wise.
40 *Quid ergo fefellit?:* How have we been deceived?
41 *Haud facile emergit:* It comes up with the greatest difficulty.

It is not intended to comment upon so many pictures nor to see them as a historical retrieval in mural form and nothing more. Taken in conjunction with finer examples upon later pages they all point towards an interpretation of dramatic

54 *Emblems originally at*
Hardwick Hall. Second
of two panels. Texts on
p. 52.

55 *Tobias Verhaecht,*
Four Ages of the World,
engravings:

a Gold *All effortlessly
fertile.*

rhetoric and give it the moral weight customarily
tied up with the visual form. Compare (30) and
(41), for example, with an emblem in *Richard II*:

That bucket down, and full of tears am I,
Drinking my griefs, whilst you mount on high.
(Act IV. i)

b Silver *Cultivation and
planning become necessary.*

ÆTAS ÆNEA.

c Bronze *Trading and exploitation appear.*

or the skull with those carried on to the stage in *Hamlet* and Tourneur's *Revenger's Tragedy* as symbols of death and moral corruption among the living. Different writers used emblems differently and the reader is wise to be on the alert for verbal evidence of emblem-influence which will give clues to the hidden language that writers employed.

A second typical art form combining both words and picture was the depiction of *classical myth*

d Iron *Violence, gaming and ruin symbolize the eternal present.*

ÆTAS FERREA.

which was increasingly popular during the Renaissance. In the sixteenth century authors were, for the first time, intent upon the development and interpretation of old myths in a systematic manner, and no successful book of mythography lacked its pictures.

An author attracted to a classical myth understood that it expressed what no other words could tell, but he might prefer to rewrite, adapt and unravel it, turn new historical or allegorical light onto it and hope to inculcate his up-to-date meaning into the minds of his readers. When humanist scholars restored knowledge of the pagan gods there was a renewed interest in authors such as Homer, Virgil and, especially, Ovid, while handbooks and dictionaries were compiled as shortcuts to all available mythological knowledge. I have chosen to demonstrate two out of a set of fifteen pictures crowding together the myths in the individual books of Ovid's masterpiece, *Metamorphoses*, a set which has not, I believe, ever been reprinted in this country. But beforehand, as a prologue, I give the sequences depicting the *Four Ages of the World* by Tobias Verhaecht (55) in which the history of man reaches from the golden state of innocence to the iron age of war and violence, which is always the contemporary world as seen by a poet with a sense of nostalgia or morality. These mythical ages act as a prelude to *Metamorphoses*, being in part myths of creation, out of which a new, continuously changing world, is born.

Picture (56a) has several highlights that call for comment. The giants piling Mount Pelion upon Mount Ossa in an attempt to topple Jove from Mount Olympus command attention. Jove reappears from the burning palace opposite. The dinner table bears the remains of a cannibalistic banquet served up by the tyrannical Lycaon whose punishment is taking place before our eyes: he is turning into a wolf, a process that gave rise to the legend of the werewolf and the lycanthropes, one of whom appears in Webster's tragedy, *The Duchess of Malfi*. Notice the couple, Deucalion and Pyrra, in the centre, behind whom heads are breaking out of the soil. They have prayed for the restoration of mankind, like Noah, after Jove's wrath and persecution. The extremely significant Renaissance image, Prometheus, who stole fire (divine

knowledge) from the gods is shown with what appears to be a blowlamp completing the resuscitation of the man at the right hand of the picture.

Smaller matters fill the picture space and readers are invited to study a text of Book I of *Metamorphoses* and then to identify Juno in the clouds and the variety of couples, human, divine and metamorphosed near the glades in a Chatterleyesque idyll. Such a modern analogy is not without purpose since Ovid appealed to many readers solely because of his erotic writing: would nonsensual writings of equal merit have proved so popular?

Picture (56b) takes another Ovidian chapter. Pre-eminent here are Diana, the moon-goddess and emblem of Queen Elizabeth herself, symbolized by the crescent-moon on her brow, and the peeping-Tom, Actaeon, whose punishment was to be metamorphosed into a stag and killed by his own hounds. Confronted by this popular myth some held it to show that lusts bestialized mankind while others interpreted it as most closely befitted their own cases. Francis Bacon, for instance, read in it that people in high office were always prey to snoopers.

Narcissus is easy to spot gazing into his pool, a scene in which one man exists in two media but still does not fully know himself. The two people killing knots of snakes are similarly but one man: Tiresias, the blind seer familiar in the play, *Oedipus*. For killing one nest of serpents he was transformed into a woman and, seven years after, repeating the action, he was restored to manhood as one whose self-knowledge and human experience were thus unique.

We should now examine two myths in greater depth because of their popularity and significance. Prometheus (57) here chained to his rock for stealing the divine fire is being punished by the eagle in an unending cycle of misery. The victim's liver grew each day and was gnawed at night by the predatory bird, the cycle beginning again with daylight. The interpretation of a man so out of step with fate and so sadly punished was wide open for a number of conflicting attempts. Bacon, in *Wisdom of the Ancients*, accepted the poetry of the myth but applied it once more to his own statesmanlike experience where men 'vex and torment themselves with cares and troubles and

56 *Ovid* Metamorphoses *from George Sandys' version of 1632.*   a (facing page 56). Book I.
b (facing page) Book III.   57 *Peter-Paul Rubens,* Prometheus Bound *(c. 1611),* 'She hath tied sharp-tooth'd unkindness, like a vulture, here' (King Lear).

intestine fears ... afflicted with innumerable cogitations.' No Renaissance man would have thought of interpreting the rocks, and not the man, as being the central feature. This, however, is what the modern writer Franz Kafka did (in *Parables and Paradoxes*), explaining that the rocks were there to teach men the pointlessness of struggling against the gods.

However, for most of us Orpheus is simply Music. The rabbit who is all ears in the engraving represents the average listener avid for the sensual pleasures of the art. Many Renaissance writers on music, on the other hand, seem to have liked everything about it except the actual sound and philosophized endlessly about it. Like the iceberg, it was the unnoticed elements of the art that caused

Orpheus (58) was equally attractive and encouraged similar latitude of interpretation. In the Middle Ages he was the philosophic Contemplative Man. Here are two later contemporaries writing:

(1) For Orpheus' lute was strung with poets' sinews
    Whose golden touch could soften steel and
        stones,
    Make tigers tame, and huge leviathans
    Forsake unsounded deeps to dance on sands.
                  (*Two Gentlemen of Verona*)

(2) insinuating the love of virtue, equity and concord in the minds of men, drawn multitudes of people to a society, makes them subject to laws obedient to government... whence follows the building of houses, erecting of towns and planting of fields and orchards.
                  (*Wisdom of the Ancients*)

These two views of Orpheus' miraculous function are as far apart as one could expect: one poetic and balletic, the other official and economic in outlook. It is as good a distinction between Shakespeare and Bacon as can be expected wherewith to confute eccentrics who feel that one man Tiresias-like wrote both outputs.

58 *Lodovico Dolce,*
Transformationi *(1561).*
Orpheus.

their greatest concern. In what follows we must throw aside our interest in 'Greensleeves' or madrigals and the lute and return to the tortuous expression of one of our last medieval scholars, Robert Fludd.

Taking first, the pillar at the left of (59). Studied carefully it resembles a one-string fiddle, the monochord. Apollo presides above *gg* and *ggg*, the highest marks on the frets and two dials (musical time and clock time) record the progress of the music in another dimension.

Centre: Note Pythagoras, the philosopher, watching the workers in a smithy who gave him the idea of vibration and pitch. It was his task to distinguish our octaves (called originally *diapason*), our fifths (*diapente*) and fourths (*diatesseron*) which were the bases of all tonal relationships. Mathematicians may care to investigate the figures, all functions of 2 or 3, which embrace the modes and scales in permanent use. Thalia, the muse, points out the modes of church music and above her head are dials, spiralling sound-waves and two porches symbolizing the ears to complete the allegoriza-

59 *Robert Fludd*,
Utriusque Cosmi. *Temple of Music.*

tion of the art and take it into the realms of the
unheard.

Right: Three towers representing respectively
the Natural, the Sharp and the Flat offer no difficulty to the modern interpreter. The short scales
of six notes (hexachords) are too complex for ex-
planation here, but since the whole sequence may
be said to lack a base-line Fludd has provided one
with a visual pun at the base of his castle which is
transformed into a musical scale of bricks.

LIBER

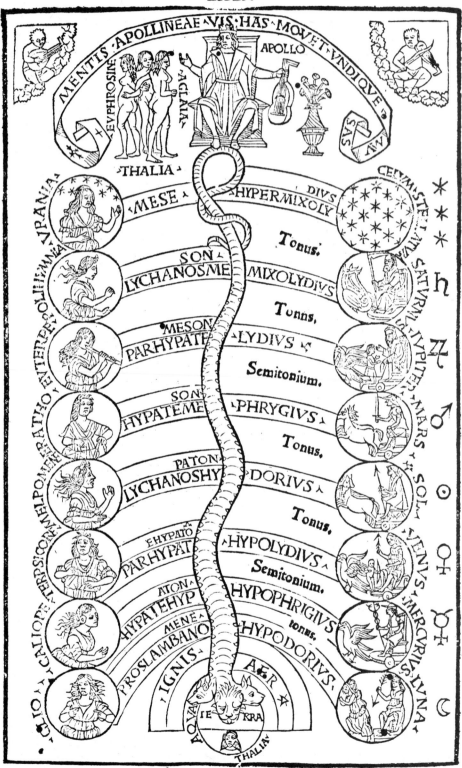

The music of Shakespeare's age is no longer unfamiliar and virtually everybody knows the songs in *Twelfth Night* or *The Tempest*. More important, in the long run, is the wider use of music in the plays. Love, hate, order and disorder, majesty and mercy all have musical equivalents and whatever was played by the performers in an Elizabethan theatre was integral to the play: none was wasted as mere background music. Its task was always to establish a dramatic mood or intensify an emotion.

In *Troilus and Cressida* appears a well-known passage:

Take but degree away, untune that string,
And hark what discord follows.

Such discord is human and needs divine assistance to retune it. Cordelia similarly prays over King Lear in these words:

The untuned and jarring sense, O wind up
Of this child-changed father.

The very storm in *King Lear* is a sound-symbol and when the old king is restored to his wits a consort of viols plays softly. Many of the symbolic attributes of dramatic music resemble the emblems here displayed and the poetry of John Donne, George Herbert and John Milton reflect the same principles of abstract or ethical music closely associated with human character.

The diagram (60), the work of Milanese musician Gafurius, a friend of Leonardo, attempts to conquer the field of the tonality of the spheres. The serpent stretching from Apollo's throne has the same role as the monochord but this time the three graces at the head are in part-control. The three-headed snake on earth with wolf- (past), lion- (present) and dog- (future) heads is an extended symbol of time; the muses in one scale and the modes (or tonalities) in the other offer a divine derivation for the whole basis of musical harmony. Thalia, the last muse—there are nine of them and one is deprived of a musical mode—is shown tuned in to space which as Marshall McLuhan wittily explains is as silent as the P in Ptolemaic.

It is outside the scope of this book to examine the modes individually. The reader of Elizabethan literature will see that the *schema* presented is a myth which tries to account for the enlightenment and sensuous pleasure that human beings can derive from harmonious music. One cannot easily exhaust the philosophical meaning that writers extracted from the art, although regrettably they were likely to admire music in the abstract but dislike the sounds it created. Robert Fludd, however, was a skilled musician just as he was an alchemist. He believed that the spheres performed scales and tones as they moved in space and the great scientist Kepler, with some reservations, agreed. It is a highly fascinating theory and D. H. Lawrence in *The Woman who Rode Away* finds it one of the last rewards for ears rejecting the modern world and tuned to primitive ways of thinking.

One piece of music may be recommended to the ears of the modern reader: Thomas Tallis's Motet in 40 parts (eight 5-part choirs) can occasionally be heard; in a resonant building it produces the wash of sound which some have believed to exist in outer space.

60 (facing page) *Gafurius*, Practica musice *(1496)*. *Modes, muses and planets with serpent Ourobouros.*

5. Christopher Marlowe

Marlowe (61), a contentious Cambridge graduate from a tough family in Canterbury, would never have fitted into the Church although he was educated for that purpose on an Archbishop's scholarship. His rejection of that none-too-pleasing prospect made him into an almost Romantic poet in the shadows of political espionage and the splendours of a world of unstable young writers. As a well-trained agnostic, pronounced in his own time an atheist, he made a formidable enemy to the religious life which he often chose as a target and subjected to critical scrutiny.

His dramatic output ended prematurely, as is well known, when he was only 29. He had been staying at the Kentish home of his patron, Thomas Walsingham, it is believed, when he was called to appear before the Privy Council. The path to London lay through Deptford and there in a notorious tavern brawl he was killed by Ingram Friser who was shortly afterwards pardoned for the crime.*

1 Tamburlaine I and II

Although there is no agreement upon the final order of the Marlowe canon of plays, *Tamburlaine* is always allowed to have been his original attempt upon the London playhouses. In what follows emphasis is given to ideas already illustrated in the earlier part of the book or to concepts that fall into a similar category. It is no task of the present writer to provide here a full critical path through

61 *Unknown Artist, 21-year old at Corpus Christi College, Cambridge, alleged to be* Christopher Marlowe.

* Since space is lacking in this book to provide a pictorial biography of the dramatist the reader is referred to A. D. Wraight's *In Search of Christopher Marlowe*. It is the most liberally illustrated biography but is occasionally fanciful in its identifications.

the play, but it is believed that all our chosen texts benefit from this illustrative technique and in this way stimulate the modern reader to a critical response.

Tamburlaine, then, proclaimed an exciting and splendid voice. With his sonorous rhetoric Marlowe designed a play that is one of the few undisputed English epics. It possesses the necessary political, geographical and historical dimensions and a hero more noted for his violence than his self-control. At the outset Tamburlaine is a shepherd, an archetype of the good life, but in his overwhelming ambition he soon leaves his rough skins and pastoral dalliance behind:

Lie here, ye weeds that I disdain to wear.

the roots of personality in the theory of the humours. He has an inner drive that cannot be allayed:

Nature that framed us of four elements
Striving within our breasts for regiment,
Doth teach us to have aspiring minds.
Our souls whose faculties can comprehend
The wondrous Architecture of the world
And measure every wandering planet's course
Still climbing after knowledge infinite
Wills us to wear ourselves and never rest.

62 *F. Knolles*, History of the Turks *(1603). Tamburlaine, possibly endowed with features of Edward Alleyn, the actor.*

63 (right) *H. Goltzius,* Hercules *shown killing Cretan bull and Antaeus. As symbol of courage he was depicted at Globe and Olimpico theatres.*

What is unconventional in this admired passage is that non-dramatic writers had no need for a war between the portions of the rational mind. Otherwise, the speech is a perfect dramatization of philosophical lectures that a Cambridge man may have heard at that time.

Beside the picture of Tamburlaine (62) we have placed the hero Hercules (63) as a visual analogy. The latter was thought of as a representative of overpowering physical presence and in the Middle Ages a typification of the Active Man, while many

Changing symbolically into the garb of a conqueror he becomes a giant storming Olympus urged on by a choleric temperament: Marlowe appears to have been the first dramatist to explore

Renaissance commentators used him also as a symbol of justice and noble heroism, a superman whose exploits were in the pursuit of the courage that virtue alone gives. Tamburlaine is not shown to have all the attributes of the Herculean, but he is similarly atypical in the lyrical utterance with which he has been endowed. Marlowe, creator of the 'mighty line' of verse, could not fail to see that in an epic poem the chief character must necessarily be given the finest speeches. To savour that poetry to the full one often needs a visual counterpart for the poetic text, as in:

> Is it not passing brave to be a king
> And ride in triumph through Persepolis?

The Elizabethan had no precise image of Persepolis, but he knew about the Triumph, the street-pageantry that was customary all over Europe when a monarch, especially a triumphant hero, visited his domains. In London the nearest equivalent available to the experience of the original audience was a royal progress or a Lord Mayor's show. Plate (64) shows a portion of a street decked out in Brussels in 1615. Many distinguished artists designed fantastic chariots for these events. Dürer's inventions for the Emperor Maximillian I stand very high in the list and should be looked at.

A favourite series of Triumphs occurred in the poems of Petrarch, translated into English in 1554. In this sequence of *Trionfi*, which were avidly seized by artists in several media, he offered Love, Chastity, Death, Fame, Time and Eternity with their captives. Mythological scenes were evoked to substantiate the moral: Chastity triumphs over Love, Fame over Death and Eternity over Time. Milton, possibly the last English writer to work within the traditions of the sixteenth century, offered a Christ in triumph in Book VI of *Paradise Lost*. Unsuitably enough, Milton's readers were able to recall the triumphal arches erected for Charles II's return to London in 1660 at that time.

Tamburlaine's triumphs took him to continent after continent and Marlowe, in the process of researching, happened upon the atlas by Ortelius of Antwerp and his map of Africa (65). Following Ethel Seaton's discovery* we can recreate the path of Techelles in Part II as Marlowe himself would have sensed it. Ortelius hid his ignorance of tracts

64 *Unknown Artist,* Triumph of Queen Isabella at Brussels *(1615). Diana and maidens in front lane, Apollo in second, ship drawn by seahorses in rear, with a fool keeping to the middle of the road.*

* Ethel Seaton, 'Marlowe's Map' in Clifford Leech (ed.), *Marlowe.*

of country by imposing small notes here and there. The mythical Amazonian warriors and Prester John are transferred into the rhetoric straight from the map and no distinct visualization occurred on the way:

> And I have marched along the river Nile
> To Machda, where the mighty Christian-priest
> Called John the Great, sits in a milk-white robe,
> Whose triple mitre I did take by force,
> And made him swear obedience to my crown.
> From thence unto Cazates did I march,
> Where Amazonians met me in the field,
> With whom, being women, I vouchsafed a league,
> And with my power did march to Zanzibar,
> The western part of Afric, where I viewed
> The Ethiopian sea, rivers and lakes,
> But neither man nor child in all the land:
> Therefore I took my course to Manico.
> Where, unresisted, I removed my camp;
> And, by the coast of Byather, at last,
> I came to Cubar, where the negroes dwell,
> And conquering that, made haste to Nubia.
> There, having sacked Borno, the kingly seat
> I took the king and led him bound in chains
> Unto Damascus, where I stayed before.

65 *Abraham Ortelius,* Theatrum Orbis Terrarum *(1570). Africa with places referred to in* Tamburlaine *marked .*

As the play moves repetitiously incidents have little or no causal connexion that can be easily recalled. We are therefore only able to see the ten acts of the drama as a series of great moments. One of his most daring deeds is to harness petty kings to his triumphal car and make them drag it along. This provides a variant upon the common pageantry in which the victims were in the background. As a piece of stage spectacle it is unsurpassed in later theatre.* It also corresponds to the archaic emblem (66) of Fortune's Wheel as the

* M. C. Bradbrook has suggested that Marlowe may have taken the notion from that cornerstone of church history, Foxe's *Acts and Monuments*, in which Henry VIII is shown standing over Pope Clement VII. The relation is somewhat tenuous but the reader will find it in A. G. Dickens' *The Counter Reformation*, which along with the same writer's *Reformation and Society*, is very much to be recommended as an outstanding example of the scholarly book replete with illustrations.

66 *John Lydgate*, Siege of
Troy *(c. 1450). Wheel,
with Fortune as 'triple-
turned whore' and poet
at work.*

symbol of tragedy, since in the Triumph all the
victims were themselves once victors and are
offered as symbols of overweening pride or *hubris*.
Indeed, Marlowe seems to have accepted the
Wheel of Fortune as a sufficient tragic emblem
where later writers parodied it. Shakespeare, for
instance, put one of his best-known speeches on
the Wheel into the mouth of Fluellen, a comic
provincial in *Henry V*, as if to say that nobody else
would be expected, a decade after *Tamburlaine*, to
see tragedy in such startling and unsubtle colours:

> Fortune is painted blind, with a muffler afore her
> eyes, to signify to you that Fortune is blind; and she
> is painted also with a wheel, to signify to you, which
> is the moral of it, that she is turning, and inconstant,
> and mutability, and variation: and her foot, look
> you, is fixed upon a spherical stone, which rolls, and
> rolls and rolls;

(*Henry V*. Act III. vi)

Where Part I ended with Tamburlaine at the
height of his fame, Marlowe had profound
changes in his fortunes to enact in the sequel.
However, no mortal conqueror was strong enough
to supplant him and it was left to Jove himself to
remove the 'scourge of Jove' and to over-reach
him. The change in mood between the two plays
gives many readers a distinct impression that
Marlowe had no need of a sequel at all, preferring
to see power without control and activity without
regret. After so explosive an opening the final
act seems conventional and dull as if Marlowe
was obeying more commonplace opinion and had
lost creative interest in his own play. The round
of Fortune's Wheel is completed but with reservations and regrets.

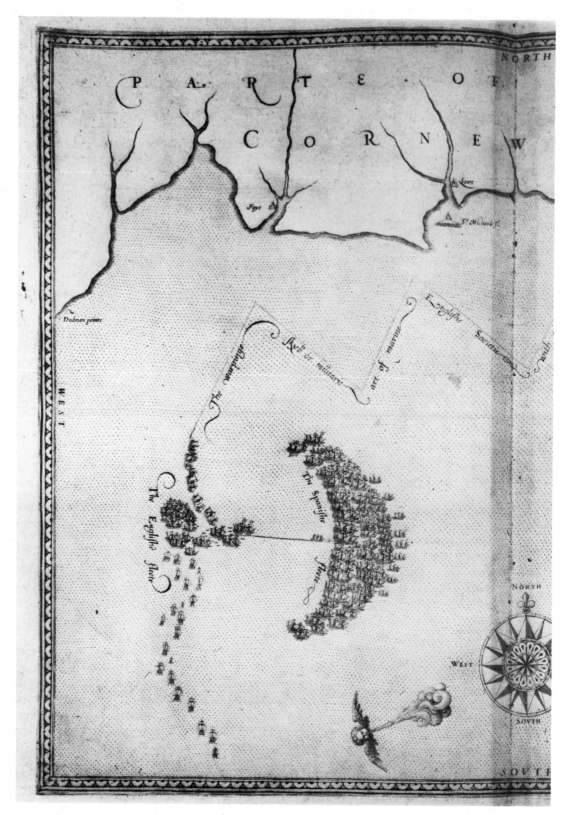

2 Edward II

From Emperor Marlowe passed to an English king and from a man of conquest to one of sorrows and humiliation. However, *Edward II* will always attract readers as an early example of a dramatic form whose popularity was greatly increased with the defeat of the Spanish Armada in 1588 (67). We must be careful not to say that the dramatic form was created by public taste at that time since it had been in existence beforehand. However, in setting one of our weakest monarchs on the stage, Marlowe cannot be accused of pandering to conventional taste. For a more family articulated type of History Play one turns to the later examples by Shakespeare but there is always room for *Edward II*, a play which foreshadows *Richard II* and even in places *King Lear*.

Though the play indeed opens with the events of 1307, Edward II's accession, the tone is far from medieval. Piers Gaveston, the king's favourite, is shown about to return from exile and planning a triumph-entertainment with which he will celebrate. It is full of mythology, a purely Renaissance court entertainment, but the departure from the traditional meanings of the central icon, that of Diana and Actaeon, is especially noteworthy:

> Like sylvan nymphs my pages shall be clad;
> My men like satyrs grazing on the lawns,
> Shall with their goat-feet dance the antic hay;
> Sometime a lovely boy in Dian's shape,
> With hair that gilds the water as it glides
> Crownets of pearl about his naked arms,
> And in his sportful hands an olive-tree,
> To hide those parts which men delight to see,
> Shall bathe him in a spring; and there, hard by,
> One like Actaeon, peeping through the grove,
> Shall by the angry goddess be transformed,
> And running in the likeness of an hart,
> By yelping hounds, pulled down, shall seem
>   to die.

It is not only that the Diana is male: this might be explained by the current trans-sexing of female roles in the theatres. It is more truly because

*67 Armada, from Library of
Magdalene College, Cambridge,
showing the crescent-moon
formation which was familiar
as Elizabeth's own emblem*

Gaveston and Edward preferred a male form. The homosexual interpretation of the old myth is central to the entire play. Like Actaeon the two male lovers will be in turn hunted down and killed by an illiberal society which is uncertain of its own motives. The old barons line up against their monarch, backwoods members of the House of Lords, still medieval figures, while the King and Gaveston are from another more modern and permissive world.

The baronial opposition is made explicit in visual terms, though it has not been possible to show their exact emblems. They stand with emblematic banners on stage prophesying in word and picture that the realm is in danger:

> A, lofty cedar tree, fair flourishing,
> On whose top branches kingly eagles perch,
> And by the bark a canker creeps me up,
> And gets unto the highest bough of all;
> The motto, *Aeque tandem*.

Corruption will eat away even the topmost branches and Marlowe uses the emblem as a prefiguring of history, tying together the sequence of events. Gaveston is first to go, but Edward, in his turn, falls from the Wheel of Fortune.

At this point Marlowe has set himself the task of enlisting the audience's support for a young monarch who has failed in the role of king, husband and, to a lesser extent, as father. Temperamentally indulgent towards Edward, Marlowe asks us to accept the man in the underground prison as a symbol of sensual man and a symptom of the human condition. He is at the last the archetypal political prisoner, assailed in each of his senses: in a dark pit he *sees* little and the *sound* of a constant drum maddens him, filth fills his *nostrils*, his *food* is foul and the castle waste laps round his legs making everything odious to the *touch*. It is an example of what was known in medieval art as the Wheel of the Five Senses and one in the tragic state of overthrow. Then when he is at his lowest, they bring the machiavellian Lightborn (*Lat.* Lucifer), who glories in the outrageous and obscene murder that he has in mind.

The roof-boss of Edward (68) shows the agonized victim and seeks to reveal the tortures he sustained—a red-hot spit inserted at the anus. To find the figure in the roof of a cathedral transforms it into an icon, precisely. After his death

69 *Rembrandt*, Faust in his Study *(1652). Source of bright light well-known in his paintings here reveals a diabolic pair of hands with Christian emblems.*

pilgrimages were made to his tomb at Gloucester and all his shortcomings were overlooked when he had become a martyr. The truest interpretation of Edward's life is not as a St Thomas of Canterbury but as an Actaeon, a passionate man creating his own destiny and fall. Marlowe seems to leave evaluation still in doubt. For the logic of history he has to be the Actaeon, yet the dramatist is equivocal and takes the path of the hagiographer showing the judgement of his saint misunderstood.

3 Dr Faustus

To open our account of this most popular of Marlowe's works we might well turn back to a picture of a genuine saint (48) and compare it with Rembrandt's Faust (69). St Jerome was famed among true hagiographers for his conversion after a life of reading profane books. Faustus, like Tamburlaine, went from rags to riches and unlike Jerome, from piety to profanity, in which mood he dismisses 'Jerome's bible'; only to pay the penalty by a total extinction at the tragedy's demonic ending. It is of the nature of the play to mix the religious and the irreligious, placing the medieval morality figures, such as the two Angels, alongside a Mephistopheles who seems reluctant to involve his victim.

Rembrandt's picture captures the same ambiguity. The scholar is interrupted in his study but is not surprised by the visitation. A pair of hands is visible and a Christian emblem within a pattern composed of the names of God. A warning skull looks in the same direction as Faustus and seems to say: 'What art thou, Faustus, but a man condemned to die?' Yet the visitation has more of the Good than the Evil Angel about it, a pleasing appearance hiding a hideous reality.

Marlowe shows one of Faust's earliest reactions as a desire to hear yet another lecture upon cosmology; his sad and almost tragic Mephistopheles obliges with one that corresponds to neither the old nor new schemata in detail. Marlowe judged his audience to be interested in

hearing an extra-mural lecture in the theatre on these topics:

> FAUSTUS: Who knows not the double motion of the planets? The first is finished in a natural day: The second thus: as Saturn in thirty years; Jupiter in twelve; Mars in four; the Sun, Venus and Mercury in a year; the Moon in twenty-eight days. Thus, these are freshmen's suppositions. But, tell me, hath every sphere a domination or *intelligentia*?
>
> MEPHISTO: Ay.
>
> FAUSTUS: How many heavens or spheres are there?
>
> MEPHISTO: Nine; the seven planets, the firmament, and the empyreal heaven.

The rest of the scene should be read with the classical cosmological *schema* open, for it contains

70 *Benozzo Gozzoli*, Rape of Helen. *Setting, dress and features make no concession to historical knowledge of the period.*

information which is partly ancient and partly modern in the 1590s, but nothing from the realm of the fantastic that such a scene might have evoked.

The final boon offered to Faustus is the celebrated interview with Helen of Troy, immortalized in these lines:

> Was this the face that launched a thousand ships
> And burnt the topless towers of Ilium?

In his source-book *The Damnable Life and Deserved Death of Dr John Faustus* Marlowe found

Helen with long fair hair, coal-black eyes and wanton countenance. Benozzo Gozzoli's picture (70) shows an example of the typical Renaissance beauty, making no concession at all to classical history. Faustus celebrates that beauty in further enraptured verse:

> O thou art fairer than the evening air
> Clad in the beauty of a thousand stars.
> Brighter art thou than flaming Jupiter
> When he appeared to hapless Semele.

'Hapless Semele' attracted Jupiter and caused him to come to her in the form of flames which killed her.* The sexes have been changed but the story is essentially the same. Faustus burns in Hell a few minutes after this interview. How far wide of the mark is the common idealization of Helen of Troy on the strength of this play! Marlowe's only comment is that Helen caused the death of his hero and he does not allow us to think it a world well lost.

4 The Jew of Malta

Where *Faustus* attained greatness as the first English version of the myth of a man seeking to control the external forces which normally had him in their grasp, *The Jew of Malta*, Marlowe's only dark comedy, reaches for a triumph of fame by dramatizing the Renaissance theories of politics and religion enunciated in its celebrated Prologue. This is given by none other than Machiavelli (71) the author of the notorious book, *The Prince*.

As the English were firmly Royalist, the theories of the Republican Florentine did not gain a true hearing in this country. Although it is known that copies of the book were circulating in Cambridge about the time of Marlowe's residence there, this would not account for the notoriety which his name attracted. Admittedly cynical and anti-Christian he saw himself as a man impelled by the truth to say that rulers were always self-seeking and cynical themselves, resorting to lies and stratagems instead of the patent honesty and integrity which was written into the official panegyrics upon princes. Quite undeservedly, however, the real Machiavelli was eclipsed by a

*Jupiter is seen above the house of Semele, about to descend upon her at the right-hand of the Ovidian illustration (56b).

fictitious one, still intensely cynical and destructive, but equated with the devil and all his works, father of all Italian villainy, and symbol of Antichrist. In his wake there followed such theatrical villains as Richard III and Claudius in *Hamlet*, not to mention a disturbingly large group of Jacobean murderers and melancholics, with never a sign of a return to a truer assessment of what the Florentine civil servant actually wrote.

Marlowe used the diabolic Machiavellian, as we have already seen, in the final act of *Edward II*, where it fitted his purpose and had the effect of increasing the sympathy of the audience with the royal victim. In *The Jew of Malta* he picked upon an incident in which Machiavelli had praised Ferdinand of Spain for mulcting the Jews in his country to form a fighting fund for a crusade.

71 *Niccolo Machiavelli (1469–1527). Florentine writer who bears a fictional image as well as a true one for posterity.*

This extortion in the name of God intensely amused Marlowe because it gave him new fuel for his own anti-Christian cynicism. It must be this trait in his writings, most of all, that so horrified an American Senator in the 1950s that the dramatist was in danger of being called to appear on a charge of anti-American activities. Other readers still more enlightened may find this feature of his plays the most attractive of all.

Barabas, the Jew of the title, is a Machiavel who is over-reached by his own servant, Ithamore, and after a series of intrigues against the government of Malta is himself caught in a trap that he had prepared for the invading Turks. There is no need to follow the full movement of the plot except to add that a great deal of sport is made with those sure-fire figures of comedy, monks and nuns, and a wholesale murder by poisoning a convent's food-supplies. This is in complete accord with the attack upon Catholicism which is found in the Prologue:

> I count religion but a childish toy,
> And hold there is no sin but ignorance.

72 *Guy Marchant,*
Kalendar. *Covetous sinners
in Hell which foreshadows
fate of Barabas in* The
Jew of Malta.

gether is the means of the Jew's own treacherous end. Who then is the greater Machiavel, Barabas or Ferneze the Governor? Marlowe used a popular folk-tradition in the delivery of the play's climax a vision of hell complete with cauldrons reserved for the covetous, like Dives in the parable, and peculiarly suited to a theatre with trapdoors (72). Yet even the echoes of that old tradition make no clear moral judgement on Barabas: he is still both hero and villain blended in one because Marlowe remained critical of the Christian's single morality and easy standard of judgement. He preferred the

But Barabas is not left as a comic figure without wrapping him in more portentous tones. He refers to his friends as 'men of Uz' robbed by the Governor to pay the tribute-money to the Turks. Yet they have no right to the emotional overtones acquired from that noble, tormented biblical 'man of Uz', Job. In such a line, Marlowe is sporting with his audience. At the end of the action the cauldron under the stage which had been made ready by the Jew and the Christian governor to-

Machiavellian subtlety, which was not so far removed from the subtlety of the Jesuits in their turn, whereby theological questions were amenable to analysis and discussion after the event.

Christian pretensions are in no way sacrosanct to Marlowe: nor, although he was a keen student of classical mythology, were the myths and meanings of the ancient gods. The Jew's servant Itha-more is made the mouthpiece for a parody of Marlowe's most celebrated pastoral lyric 'The

Passionate Shepherd', a fine piece of mis-mythology spoken by a drunken and ignorant slave to a prostitute:

> And sail from hence to Greece, to lovely Greece,
> I'll be thy Jason, thou my golden fleece;
> Where painted carpets o'er the meads are hurled,
> And Bacchus' vineyards o'erspread the world; . . .
> The meads, the orchards, and the primrose-lanes
> Instead of sedge and reed, bear sugar-canes:
> Thou in those groves, by Dis above,
> Shalt live with me, and be my love.

The legend of the Golden Age is vulgarized and the address of the god Dis is completely inverted. The gods of the classical poets are rendered comic and as irrelevant as the Christian god; useful still as sources of poetic imagery but no longer the icons that command votive offerings and deep respect.

Unimaginable as an Elizabethan clergyman, but far better educated than most who accepted the calling, Marlowe had clearly proceeded far enough in his religious education to have discovered the popular *Book of Christian Prayers*, published when he was 14 years old. In it he would have had access to a number of death-pictures derived from the long series by Hans Holbein first published some fifty years earlier. As the excerpt (73) shows, the book resembled a medieval illuminated manuscript with moral pictures compressed into the margins. From this Dance of Death he might have found his Emperor Tamburlaine and King Edward II, while as scholar and merchant the leading figures of the remaining plays similarly deserve their place. It is as if he was intent upon a group of plays in which the different social estates meet their doom and was taking his cue from the pictures.

5 Icarus

A common theme connecting the plays is expressed in Faustus' case:

> Till swoln with cunning, of a self-conceit
> His waxen wings did mount above his reach;
> And melting, heavens conspired his overthrow.

The classical myth of Icarus, a mortal who strove to fly, but was punished for his presumption, is almost as attractive to Renaissance painters and writers as those of Orpheus and Prometheus, already examined. Icarus was grouped with Ixion

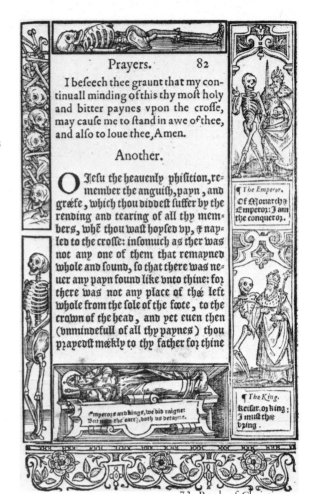

73 Book of Christian Prayers *(1578). Printing layout resembles a manuscript with Holbein pictures in margin.*

(see p. 99) and Phaeton who crashed Apollo's chariot of the sun: for the best account Ovid may once more be quoted at the moment when Icarus and his uncle Daedalus, the inventor of the waxen wings, are aloft:

> The *fishermen*
> Then stand angling by the sea, and the *shepherds* leaning then
> On sheephooks, and the *ploughmen* on the handles of their plough
> Beholding them amazed were; and thought that they that through
> The air could fly were gods.

To do justice to the event there is no need to apologize for re-introducing Pieter Brueghel and commenting on his picture (74) in its own right.

At first we notice that the painter has reduced the onlookers to a single one of each category but presumes a knowledge of the poem in his audience. The ploughman plies his craft with concentration leaving his signature on the earth beneath him and the rest are equally preoccupied with their day-to-day existence. At this point one attempts to do justice to the philosopher within the distinguished painter. He almost hides Icarus by reducing him to a pair of writhing legs as he also obscures the dead man just visible among the nearest trees of the glade. In this manner—and it is a device adopted elsewhere in his work—he seeks to show a world devoid of interest in events of significance and regardless of values. Further puzzles await the careful viewer, Could so low a sun suffuse the centre of the picture with so much light or cause the melting of any waxen wings? I know of no answer to this except to see an invisible power at work causing the Fall. Renaissance philosophers looked upon the air as the channel of the divine. Just before the death of Duncan in *Macbeth* Shakespeare describes the summer evening when 'heaven's breath smells wooingly here'. It is this impression that the picture contrives to create. The fully-rigged ship is going where? It is quite probably an emblem of salvation, but Icarus has missed this as well. The people on the rocky shore have a dangerous

74 *Pieter Brueghel*, Fall of Icarus *(c. 1560). Finest representation of Ovidian emblem of the fall of pride.*

enough existence and have become immune to greatness, so Icarus passes unlamented, unheeded.

Brueghel requires his viewer to know the myth that lies outside the picture-frame since only when armed with such foreknowledge is it possible for a complete understanding to be achieved. He was not the simple 'peasant Brueghel' of legend, but a highly scholarly man, for a long time resident in Antwerp, the chief art-centre of the Northern Renaissance, in touch with scholars in many other branches. Nor is it in any sense misleading to compare him in scope and range of achievement with Shakespeare, for not only is he the best illustrator that can be imagined for the work of Chaucer, Jonson and other poets but he has, to a high degree, developed the concept that pictures are humanist documents and, *ut pictura poesis*, like poetry, to be read.

For many modern readers what keeps Marlowe alive and exciting today is to be found in his dramatic projection of the Icarus motif in a series of compelling contexts. Some of us may, in the end, be deterred by the open-endedness of these plays, the lack of a final commitment on moral issues involved in the careers of such anti-social and alienated men.

6. William Shakespeare

Shakespeare's progress from Stratford-upon-Avon to London and from Comedy and History to Tragedy and Romance needs no biographical charting. The illustrations assembled in Chapters II and III offer instead some of the leading motifs of his work and should again be referred to when the brief studies of selected plays are read. Because of the importance of these charts and emblems in the understanding and interpretation of Shakespeare's works it seems unenterprising in the extreme that no popular separate-text editions offer anything of this type to the modern reader. Hideous photographs of sets and costumes as stylized half a century ago are no acceptable substitute: they look far more grotesque than what we would much more gladly have, the worst imaginable Jacobean performance of a play painted by a competent artist on the spot.

As readers we are concerned with our own response to the plays and it is in this respect that the language of icons and emblems may help us. We shall not in the process decide whether in fact Shakespeare believed in old or new astronomy, but we shall acquire a new impression of the imagination from which and to which he worked as an artist writing for his own time. Our beginning, then, is with one of his earliest major successes, the finest comedy written in the sixteenth century and the one with which he established himself as the leading dramatist of the mid-1590s.

1 A Midsummer Night's Dream

Characteristic of Shakespearean comedy are the themes of love, friendship and mistaken identity played out within a courtly society. Here the dramatist encircles the action with a supernatural

75 *Martin Droeshout, Portrait of* Shakespeare *from* Works *(1623)*.

background and with the forest. This is his great play of *Arbor* (p. 27), the world that dominates and energizes in the picture by Altdorfer (76), dwarfing mortals and immortals alike. Having accomplished this play Shakespeare later wrote *As You Like It* in which the fantasy is diminished but the woodland world is no less significant: this is his golden world, his paradise for comedy, and he returns to it again and again.

At the apex of the *dramatis personae* stand the immortals: King Oberon, temporarily estranged from Titania, in love with a small Indian boy—a situation reminiscent of Jove with Ganymede—the mythological characters that open Marlowe's court play, *Dido Queen of Carthage*. Oberon, with the uncertain aid of Puck, leads Titania into an infatuation with Bottom and degrades her sensivity and

76 *A. Altdorfer,* Forest with St George and the
Dragon *(1511).*

sovereignty in the process. Their quarrels have repercussion everywhere and fertility suffers:

> The ox therefore stretched his yoke in vain,
> The ploughman lost his sweat and the green corn
> Hath rotted ere his youth attained a beard.
>
> (Act II. i)

The play's second level offers the Athenian court, which is preparing for a marriage. Theseus, the only unwavering male lover in the play, is a model for the young people—Helena, Hermia, Demetrius and Lysander. Their acceptances and rejections on stage form a ballet *pas de quatre* until in the end, self-disciplined and matured by their stay in the wood, they become the model lovers for a wedding-masque, which is what Shakespeare was probably writing on this occasion.

The play's third world is composed of the awkward squad of rude mechanicals turned play-actors in the manner of medieval gildsmen on the feast of Corpus Christi. Their travesty of Ovid's Pyramus and Thisbe tale (77) brings the moon-struck comedy to its appointed midnight conclusion, celebrates the wedding with immense good spirits and contrives to satirize the author's *Romeo and Juliet* at the same time.

Filling the entire air is the world of created nature. As in *King Lear*, but for benign purpose, *The Dream* is packed with the names of bird, beast and flower. At the close of the work the humans retreat to their own private affairs and leave the animals behind:

> Now the hungry lion roars
> And the wolf behowls the moon.

77 L. Dolce, Transformationi, Pyramus and Thisbe with Lion. Notice marginal grotesques who may be commenting ironically on legend.

With everybody fulfilling his own purposes and obsessed with his own sphere, man laughs, the cosmos dances and a love-ritual play is complete.

The over-riding icon reminds us of planetary influences afresh, for it is the moon-goddess, Elizabeth's own emblem of cold chasitity, Again and again the moon is invoked:

> four happy days bring in
> Another moon; but, O methinks, how slow
> This old moon wanes. She lingers my desires.
>
> (Act I. i)

The wedding has been arranged by the lunar calendar and everything waits. However, important as she is, the moon plays no direct part in Renaissance painting. The lover with his lute in the picture by Vinckeboons watched over by a Cupid (78) might have been intended as an illustration of the play since it underlines the didactic element most strongly. It is essentially a drama-tization of ideal love and the deepening of charac-ter that such a relationship can bring to any couple whose desires indeed 'linger' for the endorsement of both ritual and society in marriage.

Standing over the sleeping lover as in the comedy is the god of love. Writers have explained Shakespeare's Puck as a deposit of English folk-lore, but an investigation shows this to be an imperfect understanding of the play. Puck or Robin Goodfellow was a gross creature who danced in

78 David Vinckeboons, Ideal and Carnal Love *(detail). Platonic, ideal and uplifting emotion is portrayed. Compare 91.*

79 (right) Geoffrey Whitney, Choice of Emblems *(1586). 'Golden Hind' circling earth, a feat with which Puck's claim was later associated.*

The didactic purpose of those lines may be said to support the other greenwood comedies of Shakespeare and the more serious woodland masque of Milton's *Comus*. In all such works it must be assumed that the audience saw some of its own wish-fulfilment and imagined that the way out of that wood was a path that they themselves should take. For the artisan and middle-class public as well as the court, *A Midsummer Night's*

magic circles with witches for concubines and not with tiny inch-high spirits called Mustardseed or Cobweb. Shakespeare most probably derived these from the spirits waiting upon the progress-entertainments witnessed by the court up and down the country, as at Elvetham (p. 11). A recent production of *The Dream* has been seen at Nottingham in which the fairy-roles were given to witches in anticipation of *Macbeth*: this is to exaggerate the slight element of cruelty in the fairies and to give rise to a further misconception. Puck is but an incompetent Cupid who makes many mistakes, yet his greatest accomplishments are to encircle the earth in 40 minutes (79) and to unite the lovers at the end. He has Cupid's flower wherewith to vanquish Dian's bud and carry to a triumphant conclusion the mistakes of the night:

Thrice blessed they that master so their blood
To undergo such maiden pilgrimage;
But earthlier, happy, is the rose distilled
Than that which withering on the virgin thorn
Grows, lives and dies in single blessedness.

(Act I. i)

Dream must have been a success, for it has never lost its power to amuse and sustain. The woodcut of two lovers (80) shows a normal audience response to such a play. They knew that comedy was a romantic form and hoped to be able to identify themselves with its leading figures.

The last picture is an oddity, thought to have been fished out of the Tiber, in which the human frame has been more metamorphosed than either Bottom or Actaeon combined (81).

2 English History Plays

While Shakespeare was occupied with the squabbles of the Athenian lovers he had in mind a larger design to show the indirect and crooked paths by which Plantagenets, Yorkists, Lancastrians and Tudors alike reached the English throne. The audience and possibly the writer may have found them as distant and mythical as Duke Theseus and King Oberon, but, either as chronicles of history or as studies in human behaviour under political stress, the plays have succeeded. Here we shall consider principally the actions of Henry IV (82) and his son Henry V (83).

81 (below) *Ulysses
Aldrovandi,* Monstrorum
Historia *(1542). Monster
possibly descended from
church gargoyles but alleged
to have been found in
R. Tiber.*

The usurper Bolingbroke, effective enough as a king, is presented as a Machiavellian racked with guilt:

> So shaken as we are, so wan with care,
> Find we a time for frighted peace to pant,
> And breathe short-winded accents of new broils
> To be commenced in stronds far remote.
>
> *(1 Henry IV,* Act. I. i)

After such an opening, peace is never much more than what we today term 'cold war', so that when Henry offers his dying advice to his son Hal it is to continue to confuse the two:

> Be it thy course to busy giddy minds
> With foreign quarrels, that action, hence borne out,
> May waste the memory of thy former days.
>
> *(2 Henry IV,* Act IV. v)

Efficiency in a ruler must be bought at this price, and with equally cynical church authorities breathing down his neck at the opening of *Henry V,* the young monarch seems to have no alternative but to open wars with France. Shakespeare's criticism of these campaigns can be found even in the heart of the epic battle at Agincourt:

> But when the blast of war blows in our ears,
> Then imitate the action of the tiger;
> Stiffen the sinews, summon up the blood,
> Disguise fair nature with hard-favour'd rage;
> Then lend the eye a terrible aspect.
>
> *(Henry V,* Act III, i)

If *fair nature* is always Shakespeare's norm, then the rest is brutalizing and damaging to the rational soul, reducing man to the level of the beast that the physiognomist Della Porta knew to lurk inside him (p. 25).

If we consider Table D, derived from a medieval commentary upon Dante's *Inferno,* and still recognized by Swift in *The Battle of the Books,* we find that societies are always on the brink of war when they least expect it. The turning point of the wheel comes at the moment of maximum security and complacency, and its workings underlie Shakespeare's view of history: no matter which régime it is, the effect is the same. Modern writers have attempted to interpret him as a writer committed to the Tudor cause. Yet compare the final speeches of Richard III with those of Henry VII who conquered him in the play *Richard III,* and it will be

82 *Henry IV—from National Portrait Gallery.*

83 (right) *Henry V— from National Portrait Gallery.*

Table D. *Wheel of War and Peace, based on idea of Luigi da Porto (c. 1500).*

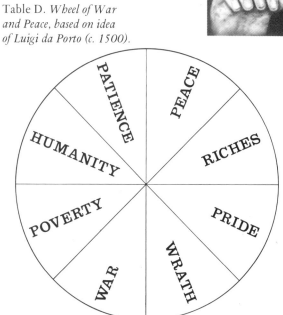

seen that the writer did not try very hard to create a convincing portrait of Elizabeth's grandfather. He was fully capable of saying under his breath 'plague on both your houses'!

A victim of this cynical policy towards human life and dignity is Harry Hotspur, a subsidiary hero of *Henry IV*, Part I. He has both his friends and his enemies to blame for his misfortune and then his fate is to be bundled about by Sir John Falstaff (84), his complete antithesis, the least chivalric of knights. In that huge frame Shakespeare poured almost nothing from the pages of history, a little of the Morality Play, in which he ranks as Riot and disorder, a little perhaps of *Commedia dell'Arte*, the soldier-buffoon and the elderly lover, and a deal of old Bacchus (85), god of wine, inspiration and comic art. Falstaff is no

84 *Francis Kirkman,*
The Wits *(1672).*
A collection of playlets that
were still acted during
Cromwellian period. Note
the earliest footlights
recorded in England.

85 (right) *Nonsuch Palace,*
Bacchus between two
Fauns. Canvas panel from
More-Molyneux Collection.

mere glutton: he is undoubtedly the most sharply intelligent person within the cycle of plays. He sees that military honour is literally an end in itself and will not live with the living; being true to his own ends he rejects it. Because he is pressed into battle willy-nilly he is quite consistent in selecting as an army a collection of drop-outs, 'cankers of a calm world and a long peace'. In that one phrase he informs us that peace can brew too long and that a new bloodletting is necessary: in other words, he is uniquely aware of the working of the Wheel of War. Chivalric fighters have vested interests on the battlefield and show no such ironic, mocking vision.

Early in Part I Falstaff asks the Prince: 'Shall there be gallows standing in England when thou art king?' In these words the speaker is—accord-ing to your viewpoint—either the voice of illega-lity or that of humanity. When he is acting the role of the king in the Boar's Head Tavern in Act II he gives the clue to the correct interpreta-tion of his desires ('this chair shall be my state, this dagger my sceptre, and this cushion my crown'). On the stage the effect can be uproarious and serious at the same time. If we glance at the symbolic meaning of the cushion that he places on his head to suit his words we shall understand him. A cushion, iconographically, is a symbol for lenience and mercy, and the reader is invited to turn on to p. 101 where Justice devoid of Mercy is exposed. Falstaff cannot give himself to supporting cruelty in the name of law and stands firm for humanitarian principles, which in the end cost him his position as boon-companion to the Prince.

For Sir John the moment of truth comes when he least expects it. Henry V, passing from his coronation in the Abbey, dismisses his old friend with the maximum inhumanity and a 'fall to thy prayers'. A recommendation to reform and a reconciliation with organized religion, the threat of an enforced good life, are too much for him. He is soon—though off stage—gathered to the underworld, to 'Arthur's bosom' where he would have been welcome, leaving his distracted friend Mrs Quickly to pronounce an elegy over him which is unquestionably the most pathetic speech in all Shakespeare's plays.

Henry V's subsequent career as a warrior is familiar to all lovers of the plays. Shakespeare, in turning the final act to a comic marriage in two

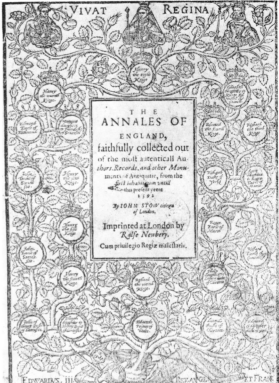

86 (left) *Geoffrey Whitney.*
Choice of Emblems.
*Bee-hive: 'A common-
wealth by this right
expressed: Both him that
rules and those that do obey.'*

87 (above) *John Stow, Annals (1592). Title-page based on biblical tradition of Root of Jesse with Virgin Mary at head. This secularized version has all the unquiet of Shakespeare's Histories and Elizabeth in the Virgin's role. A Scottish chronicle exists with Fleance at the foot.*

languages, full of double-meanings, deflates the dignity of dynastic marriage since he refuses to allow the hero of Agincourt to be seen in perfect and glowing colours. This does not mean, of course, that he was completely indifferent to the claims of dynasties and sovereignty. There can be no doubt that he preferred order to anarchy and had never considered the claims of full demo-cratic rule. His well-known emblem of the social organization of the bee-hive occurs in *Henry V* (86):

> so work the honey-bees,
> Creatures that by a rule in nature teach
> The act of order to a peopled kingdom.
>
> (Act I. ii)

Indeed, as Aesop shows us, insects have an important message for man; in the Middle Ages one would assume with St Augustine that this was the principal function of lower creatures—to instruct man how to live. But neither the wolf and tiger on one hand nor the bee on the other can teach us much. We have to live according to human principles and individuality. Shakespeare combed through the Chronicles of history (87) looking for examples of human behaviour that would make dramas out of the individual and social world of mankind. He was not studying organizations which reach a culmination in the Elizabethan sense of Order, the mood of recent long wars waiting for peace at the end of the 1590s would prevent him from idealizing the last years of the Tudor monarchy, and this is a theme to which he returns in *Troilus and Cressida*.

3 Classical Tragedies

Julius Caesar (1599) opened a short series of classical dramas which admit a number of cross-references between past and present. Most modern readers have automatically derided that scene in which the conspirators, led by Brutus and Cassius, time their oath by the notorious chiming clock. Was this, in fact, an error? Historically and technologically it was, but if dramatically Shakespeare wanted to demonstrate that human problems and manners are in no sense confined to a single culture this device was justified. It is the same with the people in the streets of Rome. Although he made an attempt to understand the thinking of his main characters as he found them in Plutarch's *Lives*, to surround them with Elizabethan citizens was another way of declaring the events of history true enough to be endlessly repeated.

The fifteenth-century cartoon (88) throws Portia's suicide into prominence. In other Roman scenes Shakespeare shows Brutus, Antony and Cleopatra emulating her. Such stoical behaviour attracted the writer's attention as a study in human behaviour outside the Christian tradition and therefore less available from modern mythology. Stoic writings were often read, in fact, by Elizabethan philosophers.

Troilus and Cressida and *Timon of Athens* are two later tragedies which feature the Greeks, a race not so highly esteemed in 1600 as in some later centuries. With much less knowledge commonly available upon the subject, Elizabethan Englishmen exercised their familiar insularity towards the Greeks, thinking them treacherous, cowardly and perverted, and this is how they emerge in Shakespeare's sources and in the play *Troilus and Cressida*. Troy (89), on the other hand, was certain of more sympathetic treatment in England because London itself was once known as New Troy or Troy-novant, an identification which helps us to understand the work. Aeneas, who appears in it, left Troy for Carthage where he met the celebrated Queen Dido, already the subject of

88 *Boccaccio.* De Claribus Mulieribus *(1473) with Portia who 'swallowed fire' as heroine. No attempt to preserve Roman dress.*

a play by Marlowe, before going on to Rome as its founder. One of his descendents, Brutus, was accepted as the ancestor of the British and the founder of London, King Lear being one of his descendents. An educated member of the audience at *Troilus and Cressida*, a play written in the first

89 Nuremberg Chronicle *(1493): Troy. The same block also served for scenes of Pisa and Toulouse. Representationalism does not call for realism.*

case for the Inns of Court and an essentially university-trained group, would have been perfectly aware of the dramatist's procedure of using one historical period as a cover for comments upon another. Thus the long drawn-out Trojan War could be read as a commentary upon the Anglo–Spanish one that was not concluded for two more years or until the succession of James I. The disillusionment with war, fortune, love and chivalry that characterize the mood of *Troilus* has specific roots in a new cynical and satirical outlook that produced, at about the same time, the plays of Ben Jonson.

For the present day *Troilus* is known for its attack upon war* and above all for the long speeches by Ulysses about Order:

> The heavens themselves, the planets, and this
>   centre
> Observe degree, priority, and place,
> Insisture, course, proportion, season, form,
> Office, and custom, in all line of order.
>
> (Act I. ii)

These words—verbose and repetitive though

*An interesting modern icon, that of Kitchener on recruiting posters pointing at everybody, seems now to be inverted into an anti-war emblem.

they are—describe the pre-Copernican universe modelled on p. 20. The phrase 'and this centre', for instance, makes a *geocentric cosmology* crucial to the interpretation. Modern writers have seized upon the speech as a statement of Shakespeare's own reactionary opinions. However, we know that Leonard Digges was a friend of his and that Leonard was a son of the celebrated Thomas Digges, the Copernican whose model is reprinted on p. 22. On the occasion of writing *Troilus* the dramatist appears to have been careful to put the Ptolemaic system into the context precisely to preserve the spirit of chronology. It is also one of the surprises of history that the Digges family corresponded with the Danish astronomer, Tycho Brahe. That being the case, can they possibly have hidden from their friend Shakespeare the name of two of Tycho's ancestors, Rosencrantz and Guildenstern?

90 *Geoffrey Whitney,*
Choice of Emblems,
*Chaos. 'The Cold and Heat
did strive: the Heavy things
and Light / The Hard and
Soft, the Wet and Dry;
for none had shape aright.'*

Ulysses, in the course of his first immense set-speech, cuts from Order to its opposite, Chaos (90):

> But when the planets
> In evil mixture to disorder wander,
> What plagues, and what portents, what mutiny,
> What raging of the seas, shaking of earth,
> Commotion in the winds, frights, changes,
>   horrors,
> Divert and crack, rend and deracinate
> The unity and married calm of states
> Quite from their fixure?
>
> (Act I. ii)

Here is a fear of universal uproar, that man's mistakes will bring about the earthquake, or 'Chaos is come again' which Othello bemoans and which is shown in its pristine state at the opening of Milton's *Paradise Lost*, crammed into a small woodcut. But for the audience of *Troilus* chaos is the entire scene, no matter how much the leaders affirm their control of events. However, at about the same time Shakespeare wrote *All's Well that Ends Well*, a comedy set mainly in medieval

France. Here the influence from the planets is described quite differently:

> Our remedies oft in ourselves do lie,
> Which we ascribe to heaven: the fated sky
> Gives us free scope; only doth backward pull
> Our slow designs when we ourselves are dull.
>
> (Act I. i)

These lines assert that men are free to choose though all are subject to the movements of the planetary and zodiacal systems under which they were born. Perhaps it was the Digges family that encouraged Shakespeare to abandon older views yet to retain them for special effect as in *King Lear* or for reasons of historical accuracy in *Troilus* where they fall less convincingly on the ear for the verbose complacency of the speaker. Finally,

donment of Menelaus show her to be a creature of sensual and not ideal love, the perfect antithesis

91 (left) *David Vinckeboons*, Ideal and Carnal Love. *Notice dog (fidelity) and monkey (lust) who incarnates degenerating sensuality.*

92 (above) Roxburgh Ballads. *Emblem suggesting 'Time hath a wallet on his back'.*

Shakespeare seems to have subscribed to the view expressed by Alberti: 'Fate holds the yoke only of him who submits himself to it.'

A sense of disillusion pervades the rest of the action. Helen of Troy, sensual and drunk, the cause of the entire war, is shown without a vestige of attractiveness. She comes on the stage calling out 'Cupid', but her love for Paris and her aban-

of the erotic spirit of *A Midsummer Night's Dream* which has been illustrated from the left-hand portion of the same picture (91). The Cupid of *Troilus* is the sensual Pandarus and its ethos is summed up by the more unpleasant Thersites as 'still wars and lechery' and the complete annihilation of human dignity and value.

The final emblem, grotesque as it is (92), shows

what may have crossed the writer's mind when writing Ulysses' long speech which opens:

> Time hath, my lord, a wallet at his back,
> Wherein he puts alms for oblivion,
> A great-sized monster of ingratitudes.
>
> (Act III. iii)

As speech outstrips any pictorial commentary, image follows compressed image:

> High birth, vigour of bone, desert in service,
> Love, friendship, charity, are subjects all
> To calumniating Time.

It is the mood of so many of Shakespeare's Sonnets, evidently his dominating experience in the period between 1600 and 1603, and it produced a play of great disenchantment and much verbal debate intended for a learned audience. There are undoubtedly a number of highly theatrical scenes but a modern writer has likened the effect of the whole drama to an unfinished study by Michelangelo: 'sometimes obscure but never tentative'. If one has seen those incomplete sculptures with great statues apparently in the act of being liberated from the block of marble inside which they grew, then the analogy is not lost. The stone is holding back the statue which seeks to get away, the former is all clogging limitation and the latter all spirit and freedom. *Troilus*, similarly, shows the most admirable qualities of Trojan idealism restrained and held back so completely by the falsity and corruption surrounding it that Shakespeare left it as his most bitter attack upon the shortcomings of both Old and New Troy, the only worlds he cared about.

4 Hamlet

The natural choice for a Danish icon is Elsinore Castle (93) because in his English plays Shakespeare demonstrated that castles were archetypal symbols of oppression, while the theatrical tradition asserted that courts and castles were the natural home of tragic events. *Hamlet* owes much to Shakespeare's Histories. The look-out platform (*left*) and the sea-walls towards Sweden (*right*) both play their part, and inside the walls

93 *Helsingør (Elsinore):*
Kronborg Castle (from
1574). Hamlet *is today*
staged in centre courtyard.

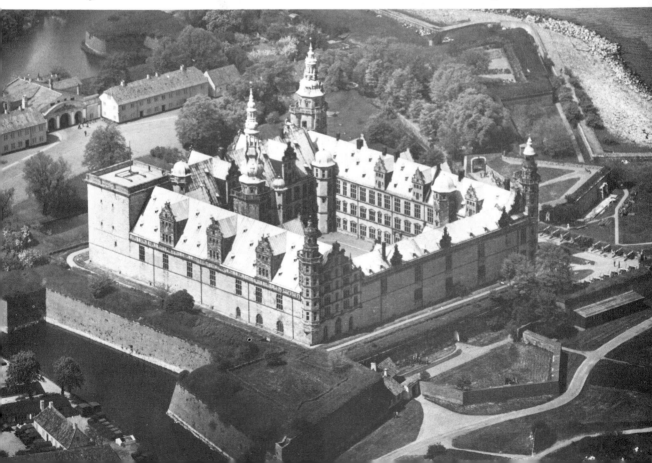

Claudius officiates. The murderer of his own brother, the Cain of the Mystery Plays, is shown instructing diplomats, spies and murderers; a dumb-show, a tragedy and a duel are given before him, while in private rooms characters ruminate on their misdeeds and tapestries are inhabited with spies. In such a world which has recently seen 'mirth in funeral' and 'dirge in marriage' it is no wonder that people have lost their bearings.

> so shall you hear
> Of carnal, bloody and unnatural acts,
> Of accidental judgements, casual slaughters,
> Of death put on by cunning and forced cause,
> And, in this upshot, purposes mistook
> Fall'n on the inventors' heads.
>
> (Act V. ii)

It is customary, perhaps, to blame all this on the King, the source of poison and murder, but the

94 *Richard Burbage (1567–1619) creator of most major Shakespearean heroes.*

For generations of playgoers the black-suited melancholy Dane has been Shakespeare's most attractive creation designed for Richard Burbage (94) to play—a male counterpart of Dürer's embodiment (32). Yet when we take stock of the bodies on stage at the end of the performance and listen to the tale that Horatio tells Fortinbras, is there an excuse for Hamlet's actions? Horatio explains:

old Ghost and Hamlet the revenger are still more to blame for turning the court into a slaughter-house and releasing a veritable *danse macabre* throughout an august palace (95). One may discover in Brueghel another vast apocalyptic Dance of Death with an entire political régime as the assailants and the populace as victims.

Revengers in Elizabethan tragedy have family loyalty as their motivation but their personal

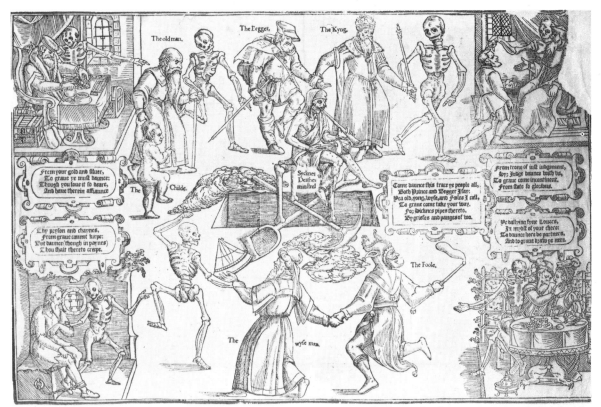

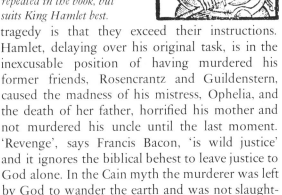

95 Woodcut from broadside Dance and Song of Death *(?1569), suitable device for much Jacobean tragedy.*

96 R. Holinshed, Chronicles *(1577). Old Warrior with armour and axe, a plate which is repeated in the book, but suits King Hamlet best.*

tragedy is that they exceed their instructions. Hamlet, delaying over his original task, is in the inexcusable position of having murdered his former friends, Rosencrantz and Guildenstern, caused the madness of his mistress, Ophelia, and the death of her father, horrified his mother and not murdered his uncle until the last moment. 'Revenge', says Francis Bacon, 'is wild justice' and it ignores the biblical behest to leave justice to God alone. In the Cain myth the murderer was left by God to wander the earth and was not slaughtered, but in the Claudius one Hamlet creates a fury on earth before they both die.

Many scholars who have appreciated the depth of Hamlet's speeches have felt that so philosophic a man must be above the brutal level of the revenger-murderer. Yet the fact that he is so is the substance of the play and many of the explanations that have been published for his delay and for his action seem to be half-hearted attempts to synthesize what is ambiguous and to rationalize what nobody else will ever fully accept about the play. Here lies the admitted difficulty of the drama and for some, including T. S. Eliot, its partial failure.

Hamlet is a backward-looking work. Much of the key action is in the past and the Prince's own hero is his father as he formerly was in life (96). The ghost who slinks away to avoid the light is not the warrior who smote the sledded Polacks on the ice. Indeed, Hamlet's father is a voice out of the past along with many other mythological names who comprise the references in the verse. One could produce pictures of them all : Jove, Mars, Mercury, Priam, Caesar, Hercules, Hyperion and Alexander, all great names out of the ancient and divine histories. The visiting players revive an episode from the Trojan War and the man playing Polonius recalls his own past when he acted in a recent performance of *Julius Caesar*, both examples of disillusionment and betrayal rather than heroism and nobility. And, as a result of this, the poetic atmosphere of Denmark is tainted. Ophelia, not a perfectly reliable and objective reporter, recalls a better Hamlet, a representative Renaissance man with all his talents:

> The courtier's, soldier's, scholar's eye, tongue,
>   sword,
> The expectancy and rose o' the fair state.

It is an expectancy that did not mature.

Alberti, the Florentine humanist, never tired of extolling the greatness of man: 'a body more graceful than the animals . . . most sharp and delicate senses . . . wit, reason, memory like an im-

mortal God.' Hamlet's books probably spoke in like voice but in his disenchantment he sees only disgust: 'man delights not me'. Shakespeare intended his tragic heroes to be fully responsible for their actions and any attempt to reduce Hamlet to a lesson in the destructiveness of melancholy is quite inappropriate. He had the understanding to grasp his identity as a son whose father was killed

and whose mother was stained, yet in his uncertainty the fate of the country is forgotten and the court is rapidly turning into a morgue. When

97 *Gentile Bellini*, Procession the Holy Cross at St Mark's *(1496). A civic and religious emblem of the Venetian Republic.*

Fortinbras, presented already as an adventurer and a warmonger, accedes to the throne he shows no sign of being equal to the task of Renaissance prince, scholar and soldier. Denmark, rotten as it is, deserved better and will only deteriorate further. The mood of disillusion appropriate to the play about the Trojan War is still unappeased for if Hamlet's Denmark is valid as a symbol for the England of 1600–1, then Shakespeare was indeed disenchanted.

5 Othello

After wrestling with the Scandinavian conscience one turns to Venice (97) with relief. It was admired in England as a centre of commerce, law, art and architecture in which oriental and occidental combine. The plot of *Othello*, based on the Turkish wars of the 1570s and the domestic life of a Moorish general, was therefore a contemporary one. Shakespeare had explored the same wealthy republic in *The Merchant of Venice* and had presented an imaginary culture called Belmont arising from the economic strength of the state. Ben Jonson, on the other hand, placed *Volpone*, one of his most disillusioned satires, in the same city and peopled it with dwarf, eunuch, hermaphrodite, corrupt lawyers and beasts-in-men. Act I of *Othello* shows a Shakespeare who has largely cast off his feelings of horror against a whole world. Iago is indeed there, but he is a Florentine, a true descendant of Machiavelli, whereas the Venetians themselves fight their wars with mercenaries to spare their own men.

Cyprus, the scene of Acts II–V, is a different world altogether. Barbaric from its proximity to Turkey, it brings out the vices in the civilized men from the mainland and subjects them to the influence of the two-faced Janus-serving Iago. The prevailing passion of the tragedy rises to the surface on the island outpost, *Gelosia* (98) with some twenty mentions in the text. Othello appears to think that he is far from jealous, only confused and 'perplexed in the extreme' from his lack of security in a white man's world, a general unhappy in civilian life and a bachelor suddenly hurrying into marriage with a partner quite unsuited to his own nature and upbringing. *Gelosia* reduces him to a barbarian and a murderer, a monster that recalls his earlier travellers' tales

98 *Cesare Ripa, Iconologia (1630): Gelosia Amante. The cock symbolizes Vigilance, the thorns spell trouble. Note the eye-ear motif as in* 1.

99 (right) *S. Munster, Cosmographia (1572). Reading left to right: Sciapod, Cyclops, Siamese twins, Ewaipanoma and Cynocephalus, all out of the equatorial wilds.*

with which he wooed Desdemona:

> Wherein of antres vast and deserts idle,
> Rough quarries, rocks, and hills whose heads
>   touch heaven,
> It was my hint to speak,—such was the process;
> And of the Cannibals that each other eat,
> The Anthropophagi, and men whose heads
> Do grow beneath their shoulders.
>
>   (Act I. iii)

He conjures up the elements in man, wherever he lives, that are best submerged. The illustration (99) captures the fears of African primitivism and at the same time symbolizes the ugliness and perversion that mankind inherited. Modern Abyssinian travellers suggest that men hidden behind great shields may have given rise to these legendary headless creatures. Thus we may have explained away an earlier irrational fear, but aesthetically would be justified in clinging to it.

The metamorphosis of Othello into a monster is

rapid. The mainstay of the state is found writhing on the floor vowing to murder his new wife. Yet Ovid's changes were ever speedy, the gods finding the dramatic moment to bring out what was latent in the man and bringing it shrieking to the surface. Actaeon was only changeable into a beast because of his innate vice. Othello, at his best early in the play, is in control both of himself and others:

> Are we turned Turks, and to ourselves do that
> Which heaven has forbidden the Ottomites?
>
> (Act II. iii)

but at the end, turned into a Turk, he intones:

> It is the cause, it is the cause, my soul,
> Let me not name it to you, you chaste stars.
>
> (Act V. ii)

The stars he names were probably part of the original stage-hangings, a symbol of heaven looking on at a murder carried out in cold blood. The man whose outlook has been poisoned by Iago is little

better than Lightborn murdering Edward II or a Faustus damned and driven to eternal hell. With a stoic suicide, reminiscent of the Roman plays, Othello ends his career.

At some point in a study which relates Shakespeare's plays with other artistic media one is bound to ask whether the recurrence of Italian places is entirely fortuitous. Up to a point it may be, but the cities of Northern Italy such as Venice, Verona, Padua, Milan and Mantua, all within easy reach of each other, force us to speculate: did he know these cities from his travels? It was a land full of the greatest artistic and human qualities; for a tragic dramatist its vices would have been a legitimate preoccupation. Experts have

noticed that the writer seems to have been familiar with local customs: the movements of the night guards (*Othello*), the evening mass in Verona (*Romeo and Juliet*) and the waterway, now disused, connecting the two cities in the latter play. The fact that he placed sailmakers at the inland town of Bergamo was always a joke to the editors of *The Taming of the Shrew*, but then a distinguished actor found them there still at the age-old task. The latest editors of the play still think it one of the writer's mistakes.

There is no convincing decision in this matter, but if Chaucer and Milton in their turn succumbed to the artistic attraction of Italy there is no reason why Shakespeare should not; if so, the opening lines of Act I of *The Taming of the Shrew* may be direct and personal, or at least at that early date a declaration of intent:

> Tranio, since for the great desire I had
> To see fair Padua, nursery of arts,
> I am arrived for fruitful Lombardy,
> The pleasant garden of great Italy.

6 Macbeth

The Canadian critic, Northrop Frye, has shown that certain images from the natural world specially fit the sphere of tragedy and give it resonance. Birds and beasts of prey assembling upon a wilderness or heath form the perfect world for such a play and one need only think of *Macbeth* and *King Lear* to realize Shakespeare's complete, if unconscious, agreement. For the former play, the most compressed of all the tragedies, he enriched the poetry with a symbolism of immense scope and variety. Some of it may have been accessible to him in existing pictorial form—such as the 'angels trumpet-tongued' whom he may have studied in the corners of old maps. Who knows what books upon demonology and magic he may have seen, not only to verify the accepted views of witchcraft but also to learn of the ritual of carrying evergreen boughs over the wintry land to promote new growth which lies behind the walking of Birnam Wood at the end of the play?

The seriousness and complexity of the play must have commended it to James I (100), patron of the company of actors for whom it was composed and who is himself indirectly involved in the

100 *Daniel Mytens,*
King James I *(1621)*.

scene the witches release from across the barriers of time eight other kings to represent the royal line culminating in James himself. Shakespeare recognized all the imaginative qualities of monarchy and the solidity that they gave to the expression of a culture. For this purpose he provided the play with royal investitures, a (haunted) coronation banquet, royal wars and a final scene prefiguring a prosperous future with the creation of a new nobility, though this might be interpreted as a satire upon James's penchant for creating knights wherever he travelled. All these factors are involved in calling James I, patron of the King's Men, the icon of the play.

Supernatural powers above the stars are evoked, a 'holy angel' is despatched to the English court, Macbeth calls upon the stars themselves to hide their fires so as not to see Duncan's murder which he cannot bring himself to call by its rightful name. Birds and beasts in this tragic universe have already been mentioned, but the animal world is not totally disordered. The long speech upon dogs delivered to the Murderers recalls their old role in medieval art as symbols of varied service and fidelity. If Shakespeare had seen a picture that corresponds to this speech we have lost it:

> hounds and greyhounds, mongrels, spaniels,
>   curs,
> Shoughs, water-rugs, and demi-wolves are clept
> All by the name of dogs . . . every one
> According to the gift which bounteous nature
> Hath in him closed.
>
> (Act III. i)

In this canine microcosm, possibly introduced because James loved the animal, one must read a symbol of human nature in all its variety; another sphere in the play's universe filled in as the cosmic tragedy grows more complete. Crows, martlets and beetles, the stones which are told not to reveal Macbeth's whereabouts, all are added until one can take the ladder on p. 27 and imagine the dramatist involving each step of it in the tragedy.

For the playgoer the test of a *Macbeth* performance comes as a rule with the witch-scenes. The women in the Holinshed plate (101) do not correspond to the description of skinny hags, and when they are first seen in their opening chorus they are agreeable enough, giving and receiving such offerings as winds for shipwrecks and the

historical events it portrays. He not only united the crowns of Scotland and England, a theme inspiring a considerable amount of writing and painting for years, but he believed that he was descended from Banquo and Fleance, peripheral prophetic and mythical figures in the tragedy. It is without doubt a king-packed drama: Duncan, Macbeth and Malcolm in turn occupy the Scots throne; Edward the Confessor, the English, and Sweno, the Norwegian; while in the cauldron

* For the Stuart family tree springing from the figure of Banquo see Part 43 of Churchill's *History of the English-Speaking Peoples* (weekly reissues).

101 (left) *Holinshed,* Chronicles, *Macbeth and Banquo meet the Witches.*

102 *From Olaus Magnus,* Historia . . . Septentrionalis *(1558).* a (below left) *'I'll give thee a wind.'* b (below right) *'Wrecked as homeward he did come.'*

like (102). It is not until the great Cauldron orgy that they act with the utmost venom and malice. The three will be within the atmosphere of the play if they begin plausibly, though one may suggest this in vain to a theatrical producer who has settled for a hideous start and may well have engaged a dozen others to assist in the undoing of the writer's intentions.

It is Lady Macbeth, as frightening as any fourth witch and as mysterious as the third murderer, who puts forward one of the greatest emblems of the play (103):

Look like the innocent flower
But be the serpent under't.

(Act I. v)

The witches should obey this same law and like Macbeth be a symbol of wickedness under a fair face to be the more despicable. But Macbeth is another Machiavellian with a conscience, like

Henry IV, and emphatically not the 'dead butcher' described by Malcolm at the conclusion. The moral hidden in his villainy is quite different and far subtler; Malcolm's earlier remark comes much nearer:

A good and virtuous nature may recoil
In an imperial charge.

(Act IV. iii)

Or, in other words, 'there but for the grace of God go I.' If the play does not leave us sympathizing with Macbeth in his last stand, his back against the wall, the reading has not succeeded. Correctly understood the play demonstrates the closeness of society and the great sweep of creation working together under an ancient firmament in which poetically we must still believe, even when the scientific revolutions of the later seventeenth century have made cosmic tragedy no longer possible.

Of flattringe speeche, with sugred wordes beware,
    Suspect the harte, whose face doth fawne, and smile,
With trusting theise, the worlde is clog'de with care,
And fewe there bee can scape theise vipers vile:
    With pleasinge speeche they promise, and protest,
    When hatefull hartes lie hidd within their brest.

The faithfull wight, dothe neede no collours braue,
But those that truste, in time his truthe shall trie,
Where fawning mates, can not theire credit saue,
Without a cloake, to flatter, faine, and lye:
    No foe so fell, nor yet soe harde to scape,
    As is the foe, that fawnes with freindlie shape.

103 *G. Whitney,* Choice of Emblems. *Serpent hiding in the Grass: 'O serpent, hid with flowering face'* (Romeo and Juliet).

7 King Lear

This is a work that is freely discussed from all points of view. It builds upon the same philosophical models as the rest of Shakespeare and draws both pagan and Christian images into its theme without either set gaining the decisive upper hand.

Lear himself is Shakespeare's most complete

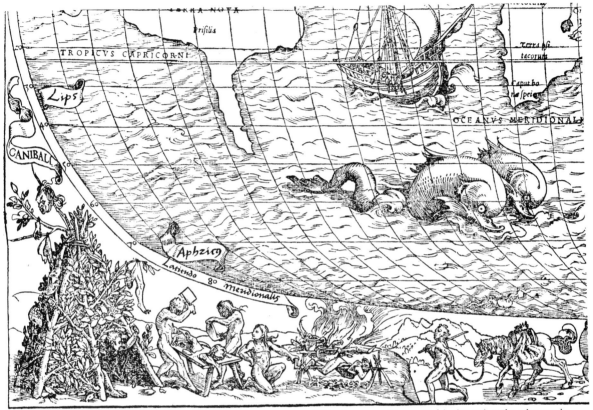

104 *Grynaeus*, Novus Orbis *(1532). 'They that make their generation messes to feed their appetite'.*

105 (left) *Rollehagien,* Emblemes *(1611). Ixion, impatient man who fathered Centaurs, half-human horses, and was punished for his tragic pride (hubris). Here bound on wheel resembling Lear's 'wheel of fire'.*

presentation of the wintry decrepitude of the last Age of Man, an amalgamation of Time and Death as on p. 91, whose icy hand causes the deaths of all three members of his family. He curses its future:

> If she must teem,
> Create her child of spleen, that it may live
> And be a thwart disnatur'd torment to her.
>
> (Act I. iv)

as well as its entire natural setting:

> Strike flat the thick rotundity o' the world!
> Crack Nature's moulds, all germens spill at once
> That makes ingrateful man.

(Act III. ii)

His vision goes even further into cannibalism when he rages against his only loyal daughter, Cordelia:

> The barbarous Scythian
> Or he that makes his generation messes
> To gorge his appetite, shall to my bosom
> Be as well neighboured, pitied and relieved
> As thou, my sometime daughter.

(Act I. i)

The scene from cannibal life, taken from the corner of an early atlas (104), suggests another range of imagery—as of a human frame wrenched, flayed, gashed, bound like Ixion (105) on a wheel or pecked like Prometheus on a rock, and glimpsed on an earlier page.

Yet Lear is not always so blind and consumed with self-pity. In the heart of the great storm-scene he learns a social insight that Shakespeare probably knew under the heading of the Works of Mercy:

> Poor naked wretches, whereso'er you are,
> That bide the pelting of this pitiless storm,
> How shall your houseless heads and unfed sides,
> Your looped and windowed raggedness defend
>   you?

(Act III. iv)

Outside the margin of this page there may have been such a picture as the *Corporal Works of Mercy* by the Antwerp artist, Pieter Brueghel the Younger, showing the compassionate feeding the hungry, clothing the naked and sheltering the shelterless. Shakespeare had presumably known of these charitable Works all his life from Matthew, xxv. 34–46, and needed no icon to remind him. Here they rise to the surface as the most poignant way of visualizing the new enlightenment that sweeps over Lear when he is spiritually reborn at the climax of the drama.

The question of Justice frequently stirs the King's conscience at this same stage in his career:

> Tremble, thou wretch,
> That hast within thee undivulged crimes,
> Unwhipped of justice.

(Act III. ii)

Because of the importance of this emblem in play after play it may be pondered upon most profitably in the dramatic realization by Brueghel the Elder (106). The operation of the law is spelled out from the time when it is in the hands of the

106 *Pieter Brueghel, Justice (1559) showing Law from document to torture-chamber and Justice herself blindfold and almost lost.*

SCOPVS LE
EIVS CAETER

scriveners until it is used as a cover for man's brutality, when every hour of the day some victim is hung, burned and tortured or, in the far distance, crucified. Look at the man in the foreground extended on the rack, water being forced into him not as a work of mercy but as further torture:

> he hates him
> That would upon the rack of this tough world
> Stretch him out longer.

(Act V. iii)

IVSTICIA

EST, AVT VT EV̄ QVE̅ PVNIT EMENDET, AVT POENA
ELIORES REDDET AVT SVBLATIS MALIS CAETERI SECVRIORES VIVAT.

107 *Ripa*, Iconologia: *'Patienza'. Thorns and yoke symbolize endurance and enshrine Cordelia's experience.*

It is the key to the exequy over the dead King at the end of this tragedy, when Kent surveys the scene and with an image from a Last Judgement asks: 'Is this the promised end?'

The entire play is not so negative as the last paragraph may suggest, since the compassion of Cordelia reasserts itself and does not die with her. Her emblem is Patience (107), a woman matured under a yoke of physical and mental endurance and capable of giving rich humanity and affection. This too is the meaning of the great dictum, 'Ripeness is all'. The phrase suggests a further combination of Patience with fields of ripening corn—and Cordelia returns to her father's camp with tears upon her 'ripe lip'—but no Elizabethan emblem has yet been found to bring both motto and picture together.

Cordelia's death may evoke in many readers a memory out of Catholic art, that scene known as the *Pietà* (the late medieval 'Lady of Pity'), in which the Virgin Mary holds the dead body of Christ in her arms. In *King Lear* that image is inverted for it is a father–daughter pair that we see when Lear has Cordelia 'dead in his arms' in the stage-direction.

It is not intended from the tone of the emblems above to suggest that the play has all the certainty of traditional religion—strong and unquestioned. Far from it. Had it not been for a questioning of the faith of the Mystery Plays, in which even the death of the protagonist on the Cross has a joyful outcome, there might have been no tragedies in the public playhouses at all. It cannot be denied, however, that such icons direct our interpretation of so overwhelming an example. There is a nightmare quality about this entire work with its different grades of madness and blindness that suggests one final Brueghel pictorial parable. In his *Parable of the Blind* he takes the old story of the blind leading the blind, which so well suits the central acts of *King Lear*, and departs from an old painting tradition. Where originally there were two blind men he has no less than six of them straddled across the canvas, elevating the original conception to one of universal and Shakespearean richness, trebling the original impact in much the same way that the dramatist did when he brought the Gloucester family and the Lear family into juxtaposition.

The portrait of Robert Armin (108) returns to the human substance out of which the dramatist made *King Lear*. It is known that Armin, the original actor of the role of the Fool, specialized in such thoughtful or melancholy parts as Feste in *Twelfth Night* and Touchstone in *As You Like It* as well as acting in the plays he wrote himself. Since there was nothing resembling a clown in Shakespeare's sources for *King Lear*, it must be assumed that the insertion of an Armin role was a tribute to a colleague of genius and an acknowledgement of practical and human considerations

108 *Robert Armin. The sole picture of the author who lived from 1568–1615.*

109 *Nonsuch Palace, Demeter seeking Persephone. Canvas panel from More-Molyneux Collection.*

within a permanent acting company that should not go unnoticed.

Armin's inclusion in the original cast of *King Lear* raises a further matter which is often imperfectly understood. It is an oversimplification to say that comic characters appear in Shakespearean tragedies as a sop to the uneducated groundlings who paid their penny. In the hands of a major writer comedy inside a tragedy had a different purpose. Comic relief in these circumstances takes on the sculptural meaning of the word 'relief', a feature which catches the eye by undue prominence and slight distortion. Armin's Fool has the effect of driving our minds from the trivial to the poignancy of Lear's situation and never of making audiences laugh out loud. As the oyster has the capacity to turn a piece of grit into a pearl, so the tragedian used the minor comedian with lasting and universal brilliance of effect.

8 The Winter's Tale

The only example to be discussed from the last plays returns to the myths of the creation and paradise for Demeter (109), also known as Ceres, as a suitable icon. She it was who saw her daughter Persephone (Proserpina) taken away from the isle of Sicily and restored in the months of summer-time. Hermione, a Sicilian Queen, loses her daughter Perdita in a similar fashion in *The Winter's Tale*. In the middle of the action she is found again in Bohemia preparing for marriage with the Prince of the country, though she is known as a shepherdess. Like a true flower-goddess she is handing out posies to all and calling on her great mythological counterpart:

> O Proserpina,
> For the flowers now, that frighted thou let'st fall
> From Dis's waggon! Daffodils,
> That come before the swallow dares, and take
> The winds of March with beauty; violets dim,
> But sweeter than the lids of Juno's eyes,
> Or Cytherea's breath;
>
> (Act IV. iv)

The clock turns back at such poetry, the imagination is again in the books of classical mythology. Such is the nature of the plot that the entire audience anticipates a happy return to her native shore and a happy reunion of all those estranged by the violence of Leontes.

Shakespeare took the story from a novel entitled *Pandosto, or The Triumph of Time*, by Robert Greene. As if to emphasize the sub-title, with its recollections of Petrarchan *Trionfi* and open-air spectacles, Time himself, complete with his old symbols, appears as a chorus to hasten over the gaps needed in the action and bring about the joyful dénouement. *Troilus* had been written out of a malicious and disruptive notion of fate and time, where *The Winter's Tale* leads all participants to a court-chapel where Time seems to stand still and bring people together almost in the manner of a temporal heaven.

Leontes, who had torn people apart, is forgiven. One who is not is the thief Autolycus, a vagabond found at the Bohemian sheep-shearing and derived from folk-lore and rogue-literature, a clever fool and courtier who is a thief born under the planet of all thieves, Mercury. For his role as ballad-monger he may be glimpsed in (110) and as a specimen of his popular wares, a piece of doggerel with a crude wood-cut, to be sung to an existing tune, the gluttony story (111) is as good as any. Like the Court Fool in *King Lear*, however, Autolycus is integral in the structure of the play and

110 *Jost Amman,* Stande und Handwerker *(1568). Stocknarr, ancestor of Autolycus, and descendant from the fool (Narr).*

111 *Typical crude woodcut in penny ballad. The subject is Kentish glutton eating his way through the waiting victims (Pepys Ballads).*

not an excrescence upon it, for the art in his ballads is a comment on the final act in the chapel.

Here, Hermione is presented as a statue which must be brought to life like magic and a tribute to the realistic powers of the sculptor. Fantasy though it is, the scene provides the only men-

112 *Giulio Romano,*
Grotesques in Mantua street.

tion in the works of Shakespeare of an artist, Giulio Romano. The writer is not fair to the visual arts, reducing them mainly to portrait miniatures as love-tokens, though he has Edgar in *King Lear* made the subject of a Wanted poster. Giulio Romano, introduced with flattering remarks as nature's rival, was an architect, painter and planner whose work was to be seen in London and abounded at Mantua.* There, he laid out the Duke's Palazzo del Tè with a complete room given over to the Titans storming Olympus, as in *Metamorphoses* I. In a nearby street, opposite the artist's own house, stands a set of grotesques and giants (112) which have an unsuspecting part to play in a study of Shakespeare's own art. Grotesques and distorted figures exemplify that tendency in late Renaissance art called Mannerist.

* Romano was not, however, a sculptor, and an art-historian has found a second Giulio Romano who specialized in painted statues. He is so little known and shadowy a figure that although he exactly fits Shakespeare's purposes it cannot be this craftsman that he meant.

The Prometheus on p. 59 with its departure from classical symmetry is but a single example.

An excellent reason for leaning heavily upon the single reference to Giulio is that originality and eccentricity are the key-note of his best work, and not naturalism. In many ways, Shakespeare's output veers in a similar direction. As in Metaphysical poetry, the words are sometimes racked with ambiguity and paradox as a result of rhetorical training, while the men and women are eccentric, mad, alienated, tragic and quite atypical as a result of deep psychological reflection. Lear, Bottom, Falstaff, Othello, Iago, Belch and Aguecheek are all magnificent eccentrics intensely affecting on a stage. 'Mannerism' is not needed as a term in literary criticism, but if it embraces such men as Michelangelo, Brueghel and Rubens, for example, then Shakespeare is spiritually at home in their company.

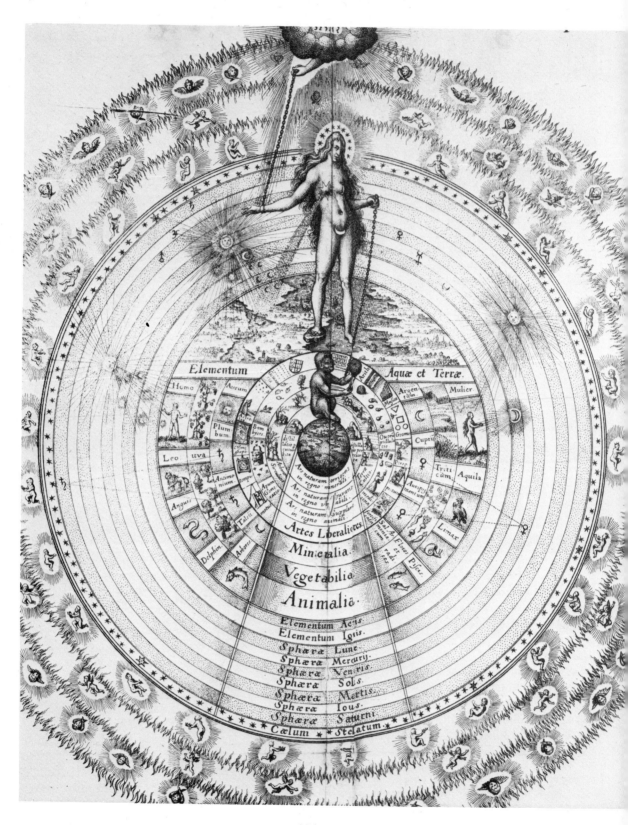

So long a divagation from the play is sustained by more than a piece of name-dropping. In Act IV Perdita and Polixenes indulge in a formal debate on the theme of Nature and Art. Perdita as a shepherdess champions 'great creating Nature' without realizing that she is a princess in disguise. Though playing at being a shepherdess still she rejects 'streaked gillyflowers', the product of grafting, an artificial assistance to Nature. Polixenes defends the process:

> Yet nature is made better by no mean,
> But nature makes that mean: so, over that art
> Which you say adds to nature, is an art
> That nature makes. You see, sweet maid, we
>   marry
> A gentler scion to the wildest stock,
> And make conceive a bark of baser kind,
> By bud of nobler race: this is an art
> Which does mend nature, change it rather, but
> The art itself is nature.
>
> (Act IV. iv)

113 *R. Fludd,*
Utriusque Cosmi.
Nature and Art showing
great creating Mother
Nature and the Monkey
(Mimesis) who creates
imitations.

The speech is full of ironical overtones and reflects a once-familiar philosophical topic reaching into many fields: what Art reorders must have been planted by Nature so that works of art are only by metaphor at all creative. A theme for Robert Fludd (113).

For his final appearance I have chosen another of Fludd's didactic schemas. Nature, 'one foot on sea and one on shore', nourishes the entire created universe. The Ape seated below her is Art and under him are all the liberal and imitative arts as well as such minor experiments as generating bees in the corrupting head of a bull, the silkworms (*bombyces*) at work, and the process of grafting again. These and many others, lost even on the scale of the original print, were justifications for the pictorial investigations of Robert Fludd.

Shakespeare, right from his own century, was called the poet of Nature to distinguish him from Ben Jonson, the Poet of Art. As we have seen, such distinctions are meaningless: Shakespeare could only render Nature intelligible by means of Art. The fruit of his study of Nature achieved permanent form only because of his knowledge of rhetoric, philosophy, mythology and much more. If it is possible for a writer to add to the store of world mythology, or indeed if mythology can be extended by any direct means at all, Shakespeare has done so, and come as close as man can to the creativity of whatever gods he acknowledged.

7. Ben Jonson

114 (left) *Abraham Van Blijenberck*, Ben Jonson (c. 1617).

115 (above) *The State Funeral of Queen Elizabeth (1603). The coffin.*

By an innate attention to detail and a thrusting personality Ben Jonson (114) realized minutely and artistically the quality of life as he himself saw it in the reign of James. His comments arise from a well-stored mind, an informed social criticism and a deep moral sense. Educated under William Camden, the distinguished historian, at Westminster School, but deprived of a university training, he was slow to find a niche and like many others towards the end of the sixteenth century he was disillusioned. The Queen had by that time outlived her own cronies and contemporaries and had never established herself as well with Robert Cecil as she had done with his father, William. At this time Jonson, ex-bricklayer, ex-soldier, writer, poet and Roman Catholic had individual cause to grumble over and above the financial problems of the country deriving from the Spanish war and the economic policies of the day. The year 1597 saw prices at their all-highest in a decade which as a whole far surpassed any other. Jonson could blame his personal lack of advancement on Queen Elizabeth's parsimony and in his *Conversations with William Drummond* took revenge by telling scurrilous tales of that long-preserved and much-vaunted virginity.

On the death of Queen Elizabeth (115), King James arrived from Scotland in 1603. To ingratiate himself he scattered knighthoods like confetti, quite ruining the landowning economies of many neighbourhoods as a result. However, he saw the arts as a conspicuous expenditure that was approved in other lands and a blow against Puritanism which he most hated. He gave his patronage to the Shakespeare–Burbage company and rewarded Jonson well. In March 1604 the poet had a hand in the coronation decorations, including the Londinium Arch (116) with niches for both actors and musicians. The central pyramid is made of stationary actors representing Gladness, Loving Affection and Unanimity (*left slope*) with Veneration, Promptitude and Vigilance (*right slope*), Monarchia Britannica, his feet upon Divine Wisdom, occupying the apex. Council, Genius of the City (speaker) and Warlike Forces between the arches and the recumbent River Thames (speaker) upon a plinth. The text that Jonson contrived for this ceremony (and what is called a *tableau vivant*) starts off with the important union of crowns now occurring:

> Time, Fate, and Fortune have at length conspired
> To give our Age the day so much desired.
> . . . beneath the Britain stroke
> The Roman, Saxon, Dane and Norman yoke,
> This point of Time hath done.

In this text may be found the genesis of the annual royal entertainments in honour of this same monarch which became one of Jonson's most successful forms of literary expression. The great map-maker

116 *Kips,* Londinium *from S. Harrison* Arches of Triumph *(1604). This open-air structure was 40 ft. high and 50 ft. wide and stood at Fenchurch Street.*

117 (below left) *John Speed,* Theatre of Empire *resembling* 116 *and seeming to capture the same atmosphere of living tableau.*

John Speed may have attended this pageant-speech at Fenchurch Street, to judge by the arch-like patriotic pattern that forms the title-page of his most valuable publication (117) and combines typography, history and even poetry with cartography.

Jonson needed an Inigo Jones as scenic collaborator to bring the great series of masques to fruition, a man who was equally a creation of the new régime. He had studied ancient Roman architecture in the works of Vitruvius until he had himself been called the English Vitruvius; he might, with better finances, have rebuilt St Paul's and refashioned the capital from his study of Palladio, Serlio and other Renaissance architects, rushing English architecture up to date in one great bound. His masterpieces remain the Queen's House at Greenwich and the Banqueting House to which we refer below.

1605 was the year of the great Gunpowder Plot, a non-event in which the Catholics made a final bid for power. It was interpreted as a mark of divine favour that the plotters were detected, as the broadsheet unhesitatingly proclaims (118). Jonson was for once silent and then, in 1612, having by that time renounced Catholicism, he produced his tragedy, *Catiline,* in which many parallels between ancient and modern conspiracies

118 *The Double Deliverance: a document in religious and political taste and intelligence.*

may be noted. He was not to remain silent upon many topics and as his role of poet and dramatist gave him ever more royal favour he became the unique writer of his age, able both to record events and to create highly individual art from it.

Because he probably designed it himself the title-page of his *Works* of 1616 (119) deserves close attention. Jonson said that 'Picture is the invention of Heaven, the most ancient and akin to Nature,' a view closely mirroring that of Leonardo da Vinci. Here, superimposed upon another triumphant arch, Jonson found emblematic form for his artistic creed. *Tragedy*, in which he did not excel, and *Comedy* preside with their different masks, dress and footwear, *buskins* for one and *socci* for the other. 'Let each type be correctly stated and fitted out' is the presiding legend from Horace. As Jonson well knew, Greek dramatic practice insisted upon exactness in drapery and

colour as a means of preserving the harmony of the play itself. Jonson was restating the old doctrine and giving it a metaphorical application to dramatic decorum.

To descend to some of the livelier detail: *Plaustrum* carries the original strolling player, Thespis, with a goat, either as sacrificial victim or the prize at a play contest. *Visorium* shows the original Chorus, while *Theatrum* matches the Colosseum in Rome with a thatched Elizabethan tiring-house. *Satyra* and *Pastora* are shown, the latter a form not attempted by Jonson in 1616 but notable for the seven-holed pipe reminiscent of the planet-bound musical art. *Tragicomoedia*, a genre popular at the time (*The Winter's Tale* and *The Tempest* are two such plays shown at the Blackfriars Theatre) is a composite visually as it is textually.

Most thought-provoking but almost lost to sight are the tiny Bacchus, complete with thyrsus, and Apollo, with divine lyre, in the topmost niches. Later ages have interpreted these two gods as the Dionysiac and the Apollonian elements in all human behaviour: on the one hand, the instinctive,

119 (left) *Jonson,*
Works *(1616). Engraved
title-page by William
Hole obviously devised by
the poet as a schema
of dramatic writing.*

120 *Pieter Brueghel,* The
Alchemists *(1558). The
line visible in the large
book reads 'Alghe-mist'
(all in vain).*

disorderly and comic; on the other, the reasoned, orderly and serious. Jonson, whether or not he realized it himself, was an unusual mixture: vigorous, overflowing and coarse in his comedy, but scholarly and fastidious in his poems, tragedies and masques when working for an ideal audience. His highly perceptive icon, not otherwise known in such a form in his day, suggests the remarkable balance inside the writer and great reason for our attempting to know his work more thoroughly.

1 The Alchemist

This is undoubtedly one of the greatest comedies of its period, but obscured for many of us because of its learned alchemical imagery. No doubt Jonson had come across this pseudo-science in a library, but he was well aware that Queen Elizabeth and Lord Burghley had both been interested

in it and that his friend Bacon held back from it because of its mixture of science with magic.

The mission of the alchemists was, very simply, to turn base metals to gold on the credible basis that there was a hierarchy of metals as there was of men, and that a ladder of metals like that on p. 27 might be imagined as the root of metallic ambitions and desires:

SUBTLE: No egg but differs from a chicken more
          Than metals in themselves.
SURLY: That cannot be.
          The egg's ordained by nature to that end,

	And is a chicken *in potentia*.
SUBTLE:	The same we say of lead and other metals,
	Which would be gold if they had time.
MAMMON:	And that
	Our art doth further,

Robert Fludd, one of the indispensable guides to Jacobean primitivism, experimented upon wheat partly because it symbolized gold in colour, a plausible belief. All he got was 'chaos' and worms, but from his further thoughts he wrote his *Philosophical Key* which he dedicated to James I.

In all this there is an unbelievable ration of greed and folly to a small grain of Promethean idealism. Turning for the last time to Brueghel (120) for comment we have the same human oddities and the crumbling homes, the vivid particularity of bottles and apparatus that Jonson gives his own experiments. We also notice Brueghel's pity for the victims, the wife with the empty purse and the children off to the poorhouse, while the master alchemist and his crazed assistant seem to remain behind in their laboratory to pursue their Faust-like urges. Jonson's characters have none of this intentness on the art and we need to turn to Chaucer's *Canon's Yeoman's Tale*, in which the moral position of the alchemists is more clearly rendered. Undoubtedly the playwright knew this poem by his most admired Chaucer (121), whom he revered as the master poet and satirist.

Jonson was likewise aware of the scientist and mystic, Paracelsus (122) who combined a belief in the divine fire in man's belly with a passion for improving medical treatment. Donne certainly knew of him and included him, together with Copernicus, Machiavelli and Columbus, in his

121 *Geoffrey Chaucer,* Works *(1598). Jonson highly reverred Chaucer.*

prose-book *Ignatius, His Conclave*, an original satire upon those who had been attempting to turn order to chaos. The Paracelsians of the play occupy a rabbit-warren of a house in Blackfriars while the master is away to escape the Plague (123). The whole action centres in this house and a small

122 *Paracelsus (1490-1541), creator of chemical and medical science still tinged with magic and mysticism.*

123 *The Plague in England.*
a (below) *Fugitives from the Plague (1630) Broadside.*
b (over page) *Plague cures recommended. Broadside.*

social cross-section of Jacobean London is drawn to it as to a bait or a magnet. Plague was, without doubt, a great and recurrent scourge: it caused loss of life, regularly closed the theatres, forcing the actors unwillingly to leave London to act in the provinces. Though the illustrations presuppose a world of death and danger Jonson allows the audience to imagine a very mild bout. A shop-keeper, a lawyer's clerk, a young gentleman up from the country and a Knight, Sir Epicure Mammon, as well as a pair of Puritan pastors, find it comfortable to remain in the city.

According to their social stations go their desires in an ascending spiral of iniquity. At the head stands Epicure and his greed to enjoy 'a perpetuity of life and lust' who is possibly typical of his class with his Ovidian imagination:

> Talk to her all in gold;
> Rain her as many showers as Jove did drops*
> Unto his Danae; show the god a miser
> Compared with Mammon.

Greed, Pride and Lust all join effortlessly with Ovid. Mammon is further obsessed by his pursuit of the Elixir of Life, the complex and mystical

* Jove's gold was thought to be a sexual fluid.

A Looking-glasse for City and Countrey:

herein is to be seene many fearfull examples in the time of this grieuous Visitation, with an admonition to our Londoners flying from the City; and a perswasion to Countrey to be more pitifull to such as come for succor amongst them, and withall.

I.
A remedie against the Plague, sent to the Lord Maior of London from King Henry the eight.

Take a handfull of Sage, a handfull of Elder leaues, a handfull of redde Bramble leaues, stampe them all and straine them through a fine cloth, with a quart of White wine and then take a quantitie of Ginger, and mingle them together, & so take a spoonefull of the same, and you shall be safe for foure and twentie daies: and so being nine times taken, shall be sufficient for all the whole yeere by the grace of God. And if it be so that the party be stricken with the Plague before hee hath drunke of this medicine : Then take the water of Scabions a spoonefull and water of Betonie a spoonefull, and a quantitie of fine Treacle, and put them altogether, and cause him to drinke it, and it shall put out all the venome. If it fortune the Botche to appeare, then take the leaues of Brambles, Elder leaues, Mustard seede, and stampe them altogether, and make a Plaister thereof, and lay it to the sore, and it shall draw out the Venome, and the partie shall be whole by the grace of God.

I I.
A medicine taught vnto King Henrie the seuenth by his Phisition against the Plague.

Take halfe a handfull of Rew, likewise of Mandragories, Feather-few, Sorrell, Burnet, and a quantitie of crops and rootes of Dragons, wash them cleane, and seeth them with a soft fire in running water, from a Pottle to a Quarte, and then straine them together through a cleane cloth : And if it be bitter, put thereto a quantitie of Suger-Candy, or other Suger, and if this medicine bee vsed before the Purples doe arise : ye shall be whole by Gods grace.

III.
Another remedie.

Take three slips of Herbe-grace, and sixe spoonefuls of Vineger, and beate the same together, then straine the iuyce out thereof, and put thereunto one ounce of fine Treacle, and one ounce of Suger, and stir it together, then set it ouer the fire, and make thereof a Sirrop, and put it in a Boxe close : then take a Sage leafe, and euerie Morning fasting, spread as much as a Beane thereof vpon the same leafe, and so eate it. And if he that taketh it, be infected it will driue it from his heart : and if the partie that taketh it Euening and Morning be not infected, it wil preserue him for twentie foure houres after.

all so plausible. The artist, although so seedy and shabby, is accepted as a guide to the economics of the future and alleged to know the entire curriculum : ('I will show you both the grammar, logic and rhetoric'). For good measure he can throw in two other arts :

> FACE : How canst thou know this so
> I am amused at that.
> SUBTLE : By a rule, captain,
> In metoposcopy (124) which I do work by ;
> A certain star in the forehead, which you
> see not.

124 (below) *Jerome Cardan,* Metoposcopia *(1658). Planetary influences upon human head.*

125 (right) *Robert Fludd,* Utriusque Cosmi. *Planetary influences upon hand.*

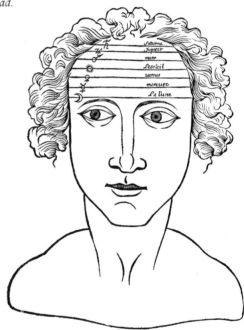

outcropping of alchemy which would erect men into the thrones of the gods and make them immortal. Mammon, therefore, voices the themes of Nature and Art with the alchemist as his typical artist :

> And thou shalt have thy wardrobe
> Richer than Nature's, still to change thy self,
> And vary oftener, for thy pride, than she,
> Or Art, her wise and almost-equal servant.

The voice of the Morality Play sounds here while the dialogue on Nature and Art is only in application different from that in *The Winter's Tale.* It is

and in the following :

> SUBTLE : The thumb, in chiromancy (125) we give
> Venus ;
> The fore-finger, to Jove ; the midst, to
> Saturn ;
> The ring, to Sol ; the least, to Mercury.

Again, man is chained to the stellar forces.

In the end, the plague subsides, the master returns and Face, the Machiavellian steward, keeps his place most politically. With its realism and its fantasy the play still forces the reader to its Morality and if it acts out one of the great Jacobean dreams it also criticizes it and uses as its scene a single house which is a mini-microcosm of the Microcosm and shows man as he is.

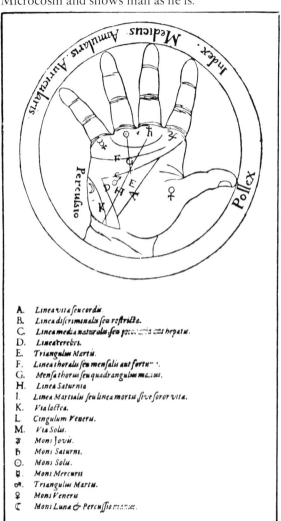

A. *Linea vita seu cordis.*
B. *Linea discriminalis seu restricta.*
C. *Linea media naturalis seu præcordialis seu hepatis.*
D. *Linea cerebri.*
E. *Triangulum Martis.*
F. *Linea thoralis seu mensalis aut fortunæ.*
G. *Mensa thoralis seu quadrangulus mensus.*
H. *Linea Saturnia.*
I. *Linea Martialis seu linea mortis sive soror vita.*
K. *Via lactea.*
L. *Cingulum Veneris.*
M. *Via Solis.*
♃. *Mons Jovis.*
♄. *Mons Saturni.*
☉. *Mons Solis.*
☿. *Mons Mercurii*
♂. *Triangulus Martis.*
♀. *Mons Veneris*
☽. *Mons Luna & Percussio mensis.*

2 Bartholomew Fair

If Shakespeare has been correctly diagnosed as a writer in the tradition of Mannerist art, Jonson probably surpasses him. The annual London fair of St Bartholomew provided him with a harvest of eccentrics in which, nevertheless, a distinct and intelligible pattern is observable. It is the microcosm moved into the open air and in default of an English painting the Flemish example (126) has so many of the necessary ingredients that we easily imagine that Ursula's delicious barbecue is in one of the tents and that the stalls are all offer-

ing what Jonson singled out for his fair-patrons on the auspicious August day of 1614.

St Bartholomew was martyred by flaying and in the medieval church his feast had been celebrated by the offering of small knives as symbols of his tortures. In Jonson's play the feast of the short knives becomes, in festive application, a carving of the Bartholomew pig.

The whole stage is set to be a holiday revel of Shakespearean richness but a serious element makes itself felt. Adam Overdo, the Justice, and Zeal-of-the-Land Busy, the Puritan preacher, represent the forces of order. Yet, since in them Jonson paid off old scores on behalf of the theatrical profession, he does not long leave them in command. What is, in fact, so remarkable is how perfectly Jonson seems to choose his victims. The Justice is typical of those in authority who, year after year, and in almost exactly the same terms, applied to the Privy Council to have the theatres suppressed on the assumption, not entirely unwarranted, that they encouraged rowdies, vagabonds, whoremongers and horse-thieves. Jonson forces himself into an awkward position of defending the theatre by pointing out in his play that the same authorities license far worse than theatrical high-spirits at an annual fair. Jonson, from what we know of his play, vast frame and his apparent obsession with the imagery of food, sides with Dionysiac forces enshrined in Ursula's tent and silences some of his characteristic moral criticism. Adam Overdo, law and order personified, is missing from his office, roving about the place disguised as a madman and caught by his own men as a vagrant. So much for the reasonableness of Apollo.

Jonson settled another old score here against arch-enemies of the acting profession, the noisier and more irrational Puritans. He had in mind those who were to become the iconoclasts, and although his book *Histriomastix* (1663) lay still in the future, William Prynne (127) is the best-known example. In that 1006-page book he reveals that plays ('pomps of the devil') were in fact enjoyed in hell each Sunday night. His mission was, of course, fulfilled in 1642 when the theatres were shut down on the outbreak of the Civil War. But even then the theatre-people had a cunning revenge. The theatres were, as we have seen, destroyed in turn, but what remained was a few illicit one-night stands in which the scenes selected were bawdy ones which most called for censorship. The greatest and most moral of dramas meanwhile languished unseen.

In the long and noisy Act V of *Bartholomew Fair* Jonson brings the entire cast forward to be present at an embarrassingly lewd entertainment, the puppet show *Hero and Leander* based upon the unfinished mythic poem by Marlowe. It is an equivocal defence of the theatre, of the sexlessness of all plays when there is but one sex among the participants. It also is made to end with a joyful acceptance from the entire audience on the stage

including the Puritan who is converted at once. In this Jonson seems to symbolize the moral worth of the drama. Indeed, he clearly believed that his art could show true justice and morality either directly in a serious vein or indirectly through satire. It was always his intention to satirize hypocrisy and greed and he ventured later to discuss such topics as patents, monopolies, the press, alchemy and many other anti-social expressions of the Jacobean citizenry. It must be admitted that the puppet-play is a hideous symbol for the drama, yet Jonson forces his audience to discuss the snares and delusions of the material world and the excellence and seriousness of the

126 (left) *David Vinckeboons*, Flemish Kermesse *bearing resemblances to the Smithfield Bartholomew Fair.*

127 (above left) *The Face of Puritanism II : William Prynne (1600– 1669), follower of Stubbes and Gosson in repudiating all forms of entertainment.*

world of art: it was the point he made on his title-page and more convincingly in the works that lay behind it.

3 Philip Massinger and Thomas Middleton

Although London led the whole of Northern Europe with its plays it did not represent the whole of England and metropolitan matters were not the only ones to merit dramatization. One interpretation of the English Revolution of the 1640s has been of country people resisting change and at variance with city dwellers, while the countryside itself was falling into the hands of unscrupulous landlords. With these problems before us from the first chapter of the book the voice of a Wiltshire dramatist, Philip Massinger, is not to be lost.

Massinger was a servant of the Earls of Pembroke of Wilton House and an Oxford follower of Ben Jonson in dramatic satire. In *A New Way to Pay Old Debts* (1621) he turned to elements in country life, where he had otherwise concentrated on city greed, and pinpointed two contemporary types. The first is the Jacobean Prodigal Son, a down-and-out from a declining family named Wellborn. His father was an old feudal aristocrat who 'Bare the sway of the shire; kept a great house; Relieved the poor' and lived the Penshurst ideal all over again. The second and more successful is the corrupt knight recently created as a fruit of typical Jacobean unwisdom. Though, as we discover, Massinger had local inspiration he was not limited by it. It was a widespread social revolution spreading throughout the shires.

In Massinger's play the new landlord is Sir Giles Overreach, an Epicure Mammon-like creature with a Marlowesque name. Massinger makes him, necessarily, a depopulator and a rack-renter. But he opens the play with an innkeeper in special fear of Sir Giles. At once the play identifies a monster of the period 1616–20, Sir Giles Mompesson, a Wiltshire knight who held the royal monopoly over ale-houses. The process of royal monopolies is the subject of Ben Jonson's mirth in *The Devil is an Ass*, written just before Mompesson rose in the social scale. Originally in an attempt to protect national trade against imports James granted monopolies as he did knight-hoods, and the possession of one allowed any unscrupulous man, as we say, a licence to print money. For his dishonest practices and his extortions from innkeepers Mompesson was fined, outlawed and degraded from his knighthood.

The role of Overreach is a firm and commanding one. It is a caricature as Jonson's are and it gains in depth by being true up to a point. Massinger was most probably motivated in his writing by the Earl of Pembroke, whose family had been patrons of Jonson, Sidney, Shakespeare and Inigo Jones, and who had political scores against Sir Giles. Theirs was not a case of old earl against new knight because the Pembrokes had only acquired estates at the Dissolution of the Monasteries, but rather the type of conflict that developed into war in the 1640s.

An unverifiable word links members of the

fortune that Jonsonian dramatic satire was available to him since it proved the stable formula with which to discuss social disintegration and give it theatrical vitality.

To advance Massinger above many other contemporaries is unfair to John Webster, Cyril Tourneur, Thomas Dekker, John Marston and the partnership of Beaumont and Fletcher, which was especially popular with the Jacobean gentry and more flattering to them than the more virulent Jonson. Space, however, allows us to take one other play, *The Changeling* (1622) by Thomas Middleton, a dramatist whose reputation has in recent years been greatly enhanced. Like Jonson he was a bricklayer's son and shared with him the position of city chronologer to the metropolis. His many plays include comedies for boys' com-

128 (left) *Lydiard Tregoze, Wiltshire: Tomb of Sir Giles Mompesson. Honour 'a slave deboshed on every tomb . . . a lying trophy'* (All's Well).

129 (right) *John Reynolds,* Triumph of God's Revenge against Murder *(1610). History IV, source of Middleton's masterpiece,* The Changeling.

Massinger family with Fountains Hall (6c) the home of another knight convicted of fraud, Sir Stephen Proctor, the despoiler of Fountains Abbey. The funerary monument to Mompesson in a Wiltshire church (128) seeks to cover up all notoriety and recalls Falstaff's cynical views of honour and glory. It was Massinger's good

panies and others in the form of social criticism, as well as masques, entertainments and this highly moral tragedy which he wrote in collaboration with his colleague William Rowley.

The Changeling was derived from a moralistic book of short tales, *The Triumphs of God's Revenge.* Each story in the collection was headed with a strip-cartoon, and as far as I know not one of these has been reprinted. Middleton departed in a few details from his original and enriched it considerably. He tells of Beatrice-Joanna who employs a murderer to remove an unpopular suitor, only to be startled that his price is her chastity.

Though the verse-texture of a paragraph by Middleton lacks the richness of Shakespeare, the structure of the whole drama is quite as complex. Not far from the castle which is the scene of Beatrice-Joanna's actions is Dr Alibius' asylum. His highly attractive wife, Isabella, commands the sub-plot and a lover feigns madness in order to gain access to her. He becomes the *changeling* madman of the title while Isabella pretends madness to tempt him. Her assumed madness contains a familiar chain of references:

> Hey, how he treads the air! Shough, shough, t'other way! He burns his wings else; here's wax enough below, Icarus, more than will be cancelled these eighteen moons. He's down, he's down, what a terrible fall he had! (Act IV. iii)

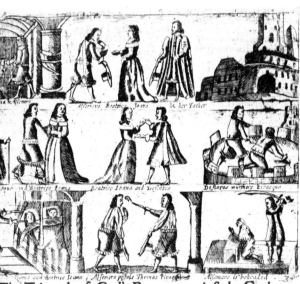

The Triumph of God's Revenge against the Crying

and the mental and moral lapses of the madfolk spreads into the world of the nearby castle. Originally intended as a firm, stable image, the castle is shown to be undermined by corruption with a pre-arranged murder taking place in its basement. The awkwardness of the engraving (129) manages to be faithful to the instability of the symbolic place and family. It is a world ruined by planetary influence:

> What an opacous body had that moon
> That last changed on us! here is beauty changed
> To ugly whoredom; here servant-obedience
> To a master-sin, imperious murder.
>
> (Act V. iii)

The person most changed is Beatrice-Joanna herself, killed by the killer she had engaged, a man whose facial blemishes go deep into his nature. Her role makes demands of the performer that would have surpassed those made by Lady Macbeth and Cleopatra but it is a principle of the Jacobean dramatist to write parts for actors, whether apprentice-boys or grown-ups, who could meet the challenge. At the conclusion everybody is subdued and changed and only the characters in the sub-plot, which becomes progressively like an emblem of the main plot as in *King Lear*, are left to the relatively orderly world of a madhouse.

Such is Middleton's *Changeling*, a tragedy now more often seen on the stage than *New Way to Pay Old Debts* which for over 200 years was comparatively popular. It is high on the list of plays that the student should know for in it he will recognize at work many of the themes of this book, the emblems, the planetary influences and the handling of symbolism in a manner that was not attained so successfully by any other tragedian after the death of Shakespeare.

8. Epilogue in Four Stages

The juxtaposition of four staged performances provides an admittedly selective insight into the reigns of James I and Charles I. It has been no part of our object to trace the political or social history of those years except in so far as dramatic literature acknowledges its pressure. Here four stages in drama correspond at the same time to the four stages whereby the Tudor inheritance passed to the Stuarts and was destroyed. A sense of nostalgia inhabits these scenes but before they each fade they have an aesthetic quality—even the last of all—which should not be ignored.

The first two are interlinked by the welcome presence of Ben Jonson. Working in the form of the Masque he found his major triumphs. The poetry poured into these entertainments was among his best, the address to the monarch which was integral to the court-masque was never before or since so well achieved; and he had a comprehending, if captive, audience before him for which he produced his best. The expenditure upon each occasion for music, costume, some 200 stage-hands, and marvels of stage-scenery introduced for the first time into the country, was borne by King James and defended against Parliament as a diplomatic necessity conforming to the European pattern of courtly entertainment. With James prepared to foot the bill—rarely less than twenty thousand Stuart pounds—Jonson was in his element.

The collaboration of the poet with Inigo Jones (130) was also essential to the success of the masque. If the latter had not travelled to see foreign stages and returned to adapt expensive Italian ideas to a temporary platform inside the Banqueting House (131) there might have been

Vandykes original Drawing, from which the Print by Van. Voerst was taken, in the Book of Vandyke's Heads. Given me by the Duke of Devonshire.

BVorstinqf

130 *Anthony Van Dyck,*
Inigo Jones *(1573–1652).*

no great Stuart masques. Many of his drawings fortunately remain, largely at Chatsworth in Derbyshire, and Jonson's texts, generously filled out with stage-directions, assist us in the task of mental reconstruction.

Between his accession and about 1612—roughly the period of Sir Robert Cecil's ascendancy—James did not excite active dislike. He was guilty, like Marlowe's Edward II, of giving jobs to the

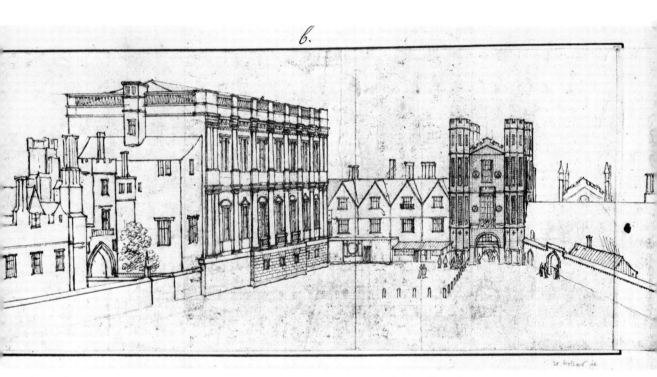

131 *Wenceslaus Hollar, The Banqueting House (c. 1640). Built in 1622 by Inigo Jones and still standing. Note contrast of Renaissance style with Tudor brick of Holbein Gate nearby*

boys, but his initial triumphs and the peace with Spain in 1604 were remembered with affection. Nobles were affronted that he had squandered so many knighthoods on the Scots, and Parliamentarians irritated that he was not sufficiently parsimonious. From this period comes the first scene.

1 2 February 1609, The Banqueting House, *Masque of Queens* (Jonson)

As Jonson's own autograph shows (132), the performance was dedicated to Prince Henry whose premature death destined Charles I for the English throne and the executioner's block. The opening of the Masque was taken up with an 'invention' of twelve witches, acted by professionals vilely accoutred and accompanied in their back-to-back dancing by uncouth and discordant music. Jonson called this assemblage of the arts of horror and disgust the 'false masque' or the *antimasque*, his addition to the form and one that could, in any other hands than his, grow out of proportion and swamp the true masque in

132 *Jonson*, Masque of Queens. *MS in Jonson's own Italian cursive writing.*

which the Good must triumph visually and morally and dance away with the prize.

The witches are shown grubbing up organs to fashion a human anew, being more malign than comic. In his subject Jonson took a cue from King James who was expert upon witchcraft and whose writings on the topic were introduced into the footnotes of the printed text. The following speech, an expression of negative emotions, places familiar ideas in a new context:

> I hate to see these fruits of a soft peace,
> And curse the piety that gives it such increase.
> Let us disturb it, then; and make Nature fight
> Within herself; loose the whole hinge of Things
> And cause the Ends run back into their Springs.

The *fruits* are the ever-occurring theme of early masques, the union of the two crowns, the perfect topic for a complimental play.

At this point, the hell-scene was rotated out of sight, and in its place appeared the House of Fame (133), designed by Inigo Jones at Jonson's

suggestion from Chaucer's poem of that name. The statues all over the front of the hexagonal structure were of heroes and the poets who created their fame, while a pyramid of ladies is poised over the double-doors. When the audience had admired the spectacle, the scene again revolved, and Fame, robed as in (134), spoke. During her leisurely speech the ladies acting the roles of the Queens (135) descended steps in the temporary tiring-house and installed themselves in chariots. At their cue these whirled into sight: eagles, griffins and lions respectively drew three triumphal cars and, to make the victory plain, captive witches were stowed into the back of each one.

A masque is not a play and it is less satisfactory to read. It has none of the causality of a play, either, so that the evil ones are overcome by the

magic of introducing more lights or playing louder victorious music or merely by saying so. When the chariot circuit was completed the ladies advanced from the stage to the 'state', the green carpeted area before the King's throne. There they collected gentlemen as partners and immediately both performers and audience mingled

133 (above) *Inigo Jones, Sketch for House of Fame. Note two figures apparently suspended upon cloud-machine aloft.*

134 (right) *C. Ripa, Iconologia: Fame, adapted by Jones for masque. Note eye-ear motif and trumpet symbolizing publicity.*

135 *Inigo Jones, Sketch for Queen of Amazons' costume, worn by Lucy, Lady Bedford, with materials 'deep pink colour, deep morrey and sky colour'.*

136 (right) *Bolsover Castle, Derbyshire, Terrace. Cylindrical decoration with plain and rusticated bands alternating still puzzle architects.*

together in the final dance, each sharing the other's world; and (since there was in the masque stage for the first time a *proscenium arch*) immediately crossing under that arch and uniting the two friendly fields.

In the years that closed the reign of James there were extravagances and scandals. In 1622, the present Banqueting House was opened. It was little used because when Rubens's fine pictures were placed in the ceilings—a magnificent set of nine pieces which also celebrated the union of crowns and the Stuart family, and are now worth five million pounds—it was not allowed to burn so many candles in the hall. James's death was a loss to Jonson, though not to Inigo Jones who was even more in tune with Charles I, a noted patron of the visual arts. Our next two scenes took place in 1634.

2 30 July 1634, Bolsover Castle, *Love's Welcome* (Jonson)

This was one of Jonson's last productions which, like his last comedies, was not a success. He had been invited by the Earl of Newcastle, who was himself a dramatist, to provide the text for a royal welcome. It would be wrong to imagine the popular furore of the Elizabethan progresses, but in the heart of Derbyshire, the 'region of ale', Bolsover was made ready.

The castle itself stands in ruins today and there is a particular significance attaching to this summer entertainment that immediately singles it out for our attention. The terrace (136) overlooks coalmines, the sources of the region's wealth.

Although it was built from 1612 onwards by Robert Smythson, the architect of Longleat, Bolsover was designed to recapture the appearance of a medieval castle needed to house troops and keep enemies at bay. It was something of a toy created to evoke the old world of courtly love and Arthurian chivalry, a testimony in stone to the English myths which had been resurrected continuously in the reign of Queen Elizabeth and re-embodied in Spenser's *Faerie Queene*. A slightly more modern parallel seems to be that of Marie Antoinette whose courtly games likewise heralded destruction.

The Flemish picture (137) shows a tilt in progress. Throughout Elizabeth's reign a tilt had been arranged annually upon November 17th, the anniversary of the Queen's accession. During these years the games of knighthood were played with absurd rules for the participants: 'He shall truly hold his promise to his friend, as to his foe; He shall be free of his hospitality; He shall defend maidens' right; He shall uphold the cause of the widow.' Under Charles I the games were still upheld.

It was one of Jonson's most astute moves in writing this *Welcome* to recall the ideas of courtly love which Queen Henrietta imported from the French court which subscribed to the ideals of 'Platonic Love':

1 Beauty and goodness are one and the same.
2 Beautiful women command worship.
2 Love for beautiful women is chaste and pure.
4 Such love is divine and all-powerful.

Could the Puritans, who knew all about Eve, possibly subscribe to such tenets as these? It was madness to think that they could, and almost equal folly on the King's part not to see that he was fast dividing the court and the country. It was, to many eyes, bad enough that the Queen was a Papist: all the old fears of 1588 and 1605 were ready to rise up anew. Add to this the Puritan views of masculine domination and their strong family loyalties and it can be hazarded how few outside the court could accept that this was a 'love abstracted from all corporal gross impressions and sensual appetites'. Such claims invite critics to sense hypocritical intrigues and Puritans to give vent to fulminating sermons.

However, Jonson knew the stage for which he was writing. Bolsover was modelled on the smaller Renaissance palaces of Italy. A Heaven Room, a Star Chamber, a Long Terrace for the banquet and a Venus Fountain for outdoor entertainment were all built into the architectural

137 *Hans Bol*, Tilting at a Castle. *Iron Age recreates Golden Age in* *chivalric game, an attempt at fresh feudalism going on all over Europe.*

plan. The masque opened with a discussion of the five senses in the Banqueting Room:

> When were the Senses in such order placed?
> The Sight, the Hearing, Smelling, Touch, Taste
> All at one Banquet?

Here he miscalculated by introducing a caricature of his former collaborator, and now his enemy, in the guise of Iniquo Vitruvius, a name too obvious to be mistaken, especially by Charles, Jones's patron.

The second scene used the Venus Fountain as background and presented two Cupids, Eros and Anteros (138), the children of pure courtly love. In mythological traditions these two were understood to be more like the Ideal and Carnal loves, p. 88, but if, to please the Queen, the only love worth discussing had to be Ideal, then Jonson found different names for them and excluded all sensuality. With this scene the masque ended and the formal welcome was complete. It is distressing to see Jonson accepting a fashion like a false platonic love as a theme, although it may be seen in his play, *The New Inn* of five years before that he had turned with renewed intensity to the art of love-poetry, as if to confute the titled lady who criticized him earlier that 'he writ not of love'.

For his entertainment the Earl paid £15,000.

138 *V Cartari*, Imagines Deorum *(1647). Eros and Anteros.*

Before long both he and the court were in increasing difficulties. Their crises came to a head in 1642 with the outbreak of the Civil War. When the Royalists were defeated at Marston Moor in 1644 Newcastle fled. On his return he found Bolsover 'half pulled down' a wreckage of the Cavalier world which collapsed gradually and ended tragically, the King rushing to his ruin speeded on by his insensitive Queen.

3 29 September 1634, Ludlow Castle, *Comus* (Milton)

139 *Ludlow Castle,*   *Scene of first performance*
Shropshire, Great Hall.   *of* Comus.

Our third scene follows swiftly upon the second but brings forward a writer whose fame was created out of his allegiance to the Puritan side. The castle at Ludlow, equally in ruins today (139), was not a creation of the seventeenth century but a Norman fortification overlooking the River Teme and protecting the Shropshire countryside against the Welsh nationalists of the Middle Ages. We are familiar with the convention that poetic entertainments in the Stuart era were created for a local event and personal celebration: on this September evening the performance was in honour of the Earl of Bridgewater, Lord President of the Council of Wales, and the masque that was seen is the only one to be at all widely known from the entire period, *Comus*. Henry Lawes, who wrote the music and assisted with the staging at Ludlow, was probably in Charles's circle at Bolsover in July before he went on to rehearse the performers. These included the three children of the family (all of whom had acted in Whitehall masques before), and he arranged the stage décor to represent in turn a wild wood, a palace, and Ludlow itself by importing devices introduced in the first case by Inigo Jones for royal occasions.

The Comus of the title had also appeared previously at Whitehall in Jonson's *Pleasure Reconciled to Virtue* (1617), a work which Milton undoubtedly knew. Milton, as a young man (140), was doubtless aware of the court Platonic circle and wrote a great temptation speech into his masque in which Comus pleads with the Lady to join such a circle of love by denying the possibility of sinfulness. She at once rejects his 'courtesy' or courtly love and stands fast for chastity.

It has been objected that the Ludlow masque concentrates so much on the verse that it has less

140 *Unknown Artist,*
John Milton *(1608–1674)*
painted as undergraduate.

time for spectacle and dance. By concentrating also on the theme of Virginity, a cul-de-sac of a topic, it may in fact be advocating the only perfect Platonic love. The Puritans knew that sin was sin and that a lady's beauty, far from exciting idolatrous worship, was a pleasure for her husband alone who was expected to dominate her and keep her strictly to himself.

Comus celebrates a true Platonic love in which Milton looks ahead to the marriage of the young Lady in the figure of Psyche:

> And from her fair unspotted side
> Two blissful twins are to be born,
> Youth and Joy: so Jove hath sworn.

In closing, let us notice that Comus himself was accompanied, as befits an antimasque, with a 'rout of monsters, headed like sundry sorts of wild beasts but otherwise like men and women.' Here in a stage-direction we may imagine a final

appearance of Actaeon in the wooded grove of Diana the chaste. The masque is not only a reminiscence of one by Jonson at the height of his powers but also of another woodland scene devoted to the reward of true love, *A Midsummer Night's Dream.*

From 1642 onwards Cavaliers and Puritans were ranged against each other not only ideologically but also in military engagement. The final months of 1648 saw a last effort by the Parliamentarians to reach a negotiated peace but there was no hope of a dialogue between them. Their charge was that the court had alienated the country and declared war upon elected representatives of the people: Charles's counter-charge was that a monarch could never be arraigned by his own subjects. Much as moderate Puritans regretted the verdict a final stage for King Charles was erected outside his favourite Banqueting House.

141 *Banqueting House with temporary stage and execution of Charles I as reported to Amsterdam. The Chain of Being in England is cut.*

4 30 January 1649, The Banqueting Hall

Witnesses of this last scene appear to have sensed that it was staged in a precise and brutal comment upon the theatre (141). In Andrew Marvell's poem, 'An Horation Ode', the imagery is inescapable:

> thence the Royal Actor born
> The Tragic Scaffold might adorn:
> While round the armed Bands
> Did clap their bloody Hands.
> He nothing common did or mean
> Upon that memorable Scene
> But bowed his comely Head
> Down, as upon a bed.

The Puritan poet goes on to notice the axe's edge, a reference, as he may have known, to the King's fear that the decapitation would be a botched job like that of his equally unfortunate grandmother, Mary Queen of Scots.

Still more in keeping with the metaphor is the account of the victim's last words with the Bishop of London, seen with him on the scaffold. The Bishop told him: 'You have but one stage more' and heard his final enigmatic line: 'Remember'.

At the moment of impact, an onlooker explained, 'there was such a dismal groan' from the crowd that a speech in *Hamlet* crowds into the mind:

> The cease of majesty
> Dies not alone, but like a gulf doth draw
> What's near it with it. . . . Never alone
> Did the King sigh, but with a general groan.

The brutalities in human Nature are for once taking their lead from dramatic Art.

Book List: some suggestions

The themes presented in the crowded pages above demand the exertions of a traveller as well as those of a reader for a fuller understanding. A visit to a museum such as the Victoria and Albert in London, to hosts of smaller provincial collections or to any art gallery in which Renaissance pictures are on display will prove quite as stimulating as the reading of further books. I have not listed here the works of the main writers of the Renaissance since if this book does not give the reader the beginning of a new way to read old plays it cannot have succeeded. It will also encourage playgoers to study the décor of dramatic revivals. For instance, the highly successful revival (1969–70) of Marlowe's *Edward II*, with Ian McKellen in the title-role, was acted upon a floor whose motif was a Wheel of Fortune and whose musical accompaniment includes a chant 'Fortuna', each highly appropriate.

It may be felt that too little attention has been given to Christian themes in the arts of the Renaissance period. It will be found, however, that in this field traditions had changed little from those of the period of Chaucer, some of which will be shown in the present author's *Chaucer's World* (Cambridge University Press) and many more in Emile Mâle's *Gothic Image* (Fontana Library).

The bibliography that follows is extremely varied but few of the books, it should be noted, are for the complete beginner.

James Ackerman, *Andrea Palladio*, Penguin.

F. B. Artz, *Renaissance to Reformation*, Chicago Univ. Press.

Otto Benesch, *The Art of the Renaissance in Northern Europe*, Phaidon.

S. C. Chew, *The Pilgrimage of Life*, Yale Univ. Press.

J. G. Demaray, *Milton and the Masque Tradition*, Harvard Univ. Press.

A. G. Dickens, *The Counter Reformation*, Thames and Hudson.

— *Reformation and Society*, Thames and Hudson.

P. L. Duchartre, *The Italian Comedy*, Dover Books.

Rosemary Freeman, *English Emblem Books*, Chatto and Windus.

P. Hartnoll (Ed.), *The Oxford Companion to the Theatre*, Oxford Univ. Press.

A. J. Meadows, *The High Firmament*, Leicester Univ. Press.

Allardyce Nicoll, *The Elizabethans*, Cambridge Univ. Press.

Stephen Orgel, *Ben Jonson's Masques*, Yale Univ. Press.

Edith Rickert, *Painting in Britain*, Penguin.

Jean Seznec, *Survival of the Pagan Gods*, Harper.

Richard Southern, *Seven Ages of Theatre*, Faber.

John Summerson, *Architecture in Britain*, Penguin.

— *Inigo Jones*, Penguin.

Glynne Wickham, *Early English Stages*, II, Routledge.

— *Shakespeare's Dramatic Heritage*, Routledge.

Edgar Wind, *Pagan Mysteries of the Renaissance*, Faber.

James Winny, *Preface to Donne*, Longman.

Rudolf Wittkower, *Architectural Principles in the Age of Humanism*, Tiranti.

Finally, the reader is urged to go to as many parts of the country as he can looking for well-preserved relics of the Elizabethan past. Several suitable towns have already been mentioned and illustrated. A special case may be made here for the Kentish town of Faversham. In 1550, Arden, the mayor, was murdered by his wife's lover. The story merited five pages in Holinshed and attracted the author of the finest anonymous Elizabethan tragedy, *Arden of Feversham*. The house itself may be visited as one of many attractive Tudor houses in a town on the way to Marlowe's Canterbury. Apart from the most obvious cathedral and university centres it is impossible to list the eligible spots to seek out. The habit of consulting the indispensable Penguin series, *The Buildings of England* by Sir Nikolaus Pevsner, is one that cannot be bettered.

Index

References in bold figures refer to page numbers of illustrations

Index